WHIRLWINDS OF GOD

Messages
by
ROBERT G. LEE, D.D., LL.D., LITT. D.
Pastor, Bellevue Baptist Church
Memphis, Tennessee

ZONDERVAN

ZONDERVAN PUBLISHING HOUSE
GRAND RAPIDS, MICHIGAN

Published by
ZONDERVAN PUBLISHING HOUSE
Grand Rapids, Michigan

TO

BELLEVUE BAPTIST CHURCH

—"Dearly beloved and longed for,
my joy and crown . . . my dearly beloved,"
whose *follow*ship has made effective in
Memphis the pastor's *leader*ship for
Jesus Christ—

TO THIS GREAT CHURCH

this volume is dedicated by the author.

"I thank God upon every remembrance of you."

19851

CONTENTS

CHAPTER 1

THE WHIRLWINDS OF GOD

The Lord hath his way in the whirlwind (Nahum 1:3).

All the prophecies in the book of Nahum pertain to Nineveh.

Nahum lived and prophesied from 664 B.C. to 607 B.C.—approximately. (The expression "before Christ" refers to the years before Christ was made flesh, for "he was before all things" (Col. 1:17) and He had glory with the Father "before the world was" (John 17:5).

The book of Nahum is chiefly a sequel to the book of Jonah. Both Nahum and Jonah had their minds and hearts stirred by pondering and presenting God's message to Nineveh—"Nineveh, that great city" (Jonah 1:2); Nineveh, "an exceeding great city of three days' journey" (Jonah 3:3); Nineveh, "wherein are more than sixscore thousand persons that could not discern between their right hand and their left" (Jonah 4:11); Nineveh, surrounded by walls which were one hundred feet high and surmounted by two hundred towers.

Jonah, with pungent and fiery repetition, had already warned Nineveh concerning her wickedness and of the impending punishments of God—punishments which God remitted when Nineveh repented. Nahum now repeats these denunciations. The one theme of his prophecy is the destruction of Nineveh—Nineveh then at the height of its power, the noonday of her pride, the midnight of her sin, and the depths of her degradation.

In the chapter in which we find the majesty of God's goodness to His people and the severity of God against His adversaries so beautifully portrayed, we also find our text gleaming like a pearl amid pearls—"The Lord hath his way in the whirlwind." We can learn much truth from God by thinking upon what the Bible reveals in connection with its mention of whirlwinds. May the truth we learn help us to serve Him who "hath made the earth by his power, . . . causeth the vapours to ascend from the ends of the earth: he maketh lightnings with rain, and bringeth forth the wind out of his treasures" (Jeremiah 51:15, 16).

WHIRLWINDS OF GOD

I. THE WHIRLWINDS OF GOD SPEAK OF HIS ETERNITY

Behold, the whirlwind of the Lord goeth forth with fury, a continuing whirlwind (Jeremiah 30:23).

A *continuing* whirlwind! A *ceaseless* whirlwind. An ever active whirlwind. A whirlwind active when the flowers and fruits of summer are in the land. A continuing whirlwind when the fires of autumn are burning over hill and vale. A continuing whirlwind when the snows of winter cover the earth. A continuing whirlwind in spring, when God weaves a mystic skein over cragmoor, hill and plain. A *continuing* whirlwind—showing forth the eternity of God, testifying to his ceaseless activity in the universe.

Now unto the King eternal, immortal, invisible, the only wise God, be honour and glory for ever and ever (I Timothy 1:17).

Before the mountains were brought forth, or ever thou hadst formed the earth and the world, even from everlasting to everlasting, thou art God (Psalm 90:2).

But thou, O Lord shalt endure for ever, and thy remembrance unto all generations (Psalm 102:12).

Hast thou not known? hast thou not heard, that the everlasting

God, the Lord, the Creator of the ends of the earth, fainteth not, neither is weary (Isaiah 40:28).

Blessed be the Lord God of Israel from everlasting, and to everlasting (Psalm 41:13).

To this, the eternity of God, the *continuing* whirlwind of the Lord gives testimony in symbolic significance.

The eternity of God is duration without beginning or end—a *continuing* fact. The eternity of God is existence without bound or dimension—a *continuing* existence. The eternity of God is present, without past or future—a *continuing* present. God's eternity is youth without infancy, youth without old age. God's eternity, his *continuing* existence, is life without birth, life without death. God's eternity is today—today without yesterday, today without tomorrow. He is the unchangeable God. Nations go. God remains. Above the graves and tombs of all nations God reigns. God—"the same yesterday, today, and for ever" (Hebrews 13:8). God—"with whom is no variableness, neither shadow of turning" (James 1:17). There is never a wrinkle on the brow of God. Forever he is the God who neither fainteth nor is weary. God is where He first was. He continues forever a God of eternal and infinite power—able, willing, mighty to save those who trust in him, powerful to help us in our perplexities. His goodness never fails to guide us in our gloom and His hand holds out help to us in our hazards.

God is the first cause—absolutely. God is the first cause—universally. God is the first cause—everlastingly. If we back track science, we will arrive at the mind of God. If we look back and trace moral principles, we will arrive at God's character. If we count all the years that lie in the tomb of time and trace back existence, we will arrive at God's existence. What He was, He is. What He will be, He ever has been. He changes not. We cannot say that too often. Essentially God is immutable. His essence asserts so much. His laws assert so much. His government asserts so much. Christianity asserts so much. That is what Jeremiah meant when he spoke of "the whirlwind of the Lord . . . a *continuing* whirlwind."

God's immutability and eternity are pledged for the perpetuity of his church. Originally the church was built upon Christ. Never has it been shifted from its foundation. Never can it be. Never will it be. Never.

Somebody gave us volumes of truth in a few lines, gave us acres of truth in inches of language, gave us rivers of religious reality in a rill of speech, who said:

"See that huge granite boulder heaved by volcanic power from some mountain's side, lying upon the ocean's shore amid the accumulated debris of the centuries, exhibiting the abrasions of tides and drifts, worn by winds and driving rains, and scarred and cracked by the heavy tramp of ages? Even its indurated structure has not been able to resist the power of change. But the church of God, uncorroded by the teeth of flying years, unmarked by the fragments of thrones and republics continually drifting by on the roaring current of time and unbattered by the infringement and concussion of hell's infernal thunderbolts—lifts its walls and turrets in unscathed and imperishable strength to heaven, as impregnable as the throne of God!"

Which is just another way of emphasizing what Jesus said when he made the assertion that the gates of hell should never prevail against his church (Matthew 16:18). Such truth gives us assurance that drives away fears. Such assurance delivers our hands from weariness in well-doing. Such assurance gives our feet faithfulness in following where he leads. Such assurance delivers our hearts from fainting. Such assurance gives our shoulders strength for burden-bearing. Such assurance keeps us from thinking that *all* is lost when *one* battle is lost. Yes, such assurance comforts us and strengthens us, not only concerning the work and mission of the church, but comforts and strengthens us for individual life.

This comfort and strength gives us victory over the fear that often comes when we think of eternity, and for the hour when we face eternity—"eternity whose incalculable and incomprehensible value no subtraction can diminish, whose incalculable and incomprehensible value no addition can increase." I think one of our recent poets has expressed this beautifully in the poem "Fear". Youth speaks and age speaks.

Youth says:

> The night is dark; the wind is still;
> A hound bays on a distant hill;
> The world is large!—and I am small;
> My path is veiled—ah, I shall fall!
> O Mother, let me have your hand!

Age declares:

> The night is black; the wind is shrill;
> The hounds bay on a closer hill;
> Oh, larger world! and I so small!
> Eternity—one long, last call—
> My God, my God, give me Thy hand!

With the hand of the eternal God upon ours, we can face eternity fearlessly—eternity in whose awful shadow all worlds, men, angels, and devils perform their parts. Yes, with the hand of Him who hath His way in the whirlwind—a *continuing* whirlwind—we can face eternity with the joy of a little child who goes out to play, with the dignity of a king who goes forth to coronation.

II. The Whirlwinds of God Testify That God Has Answers for Man's Questions

Then the Lord answered Job out of the whirlwind (Job 38:1).
God answered Job out of the whirlwind (Job 40:6).

Only God has an answer for every question of man.

Man says, "I have life—what shall I do with it?" And God answers, "In all thy ways acknowledge him, and he shall direct thy paths" (Proverbs 3:6). "The Lord is the strength of my life; of whom shall I be afraid?" (Psalms 27:1).

Give your life to God. God is the fashioner of royal character, and in His hand the reed which is shaken by the wind is transformed into an iron pillar which cannot be moved. Give your life to God. Put it on His altar. Put it to His ploughshare. Your mind will be established in the truth of God. Your heart will be confirmed in the purpose of God. Your will will be possessed by the holy strength of God. You will confront all hostilities without breaking, bending or yielding—invincible before the onslaughts of the world, the flesh, the devil. You will be able to stand against all enervating airs from the South. You will be able to stand against all fierce blasts from the icy North. That is part of the answer God gives to the man who says, "What shall I do with my life?"

But man asks a harder question, "What shall I do with my sins?" God, God alone, has the answer for that tragic question. As I turn the pages of Holy Writ, I find that question asked again and again, echoed again and again, sobbed again and again, uttered with lamentation again and again, wailed with intonations of misery over and over. Generation after generation asks that question. Age after age after age asks that question. The stoic asks it. The philosopher asks it. The scholar asks it. The saint asks it. The savage asks it in one way and another. Yet, aside from God, never once has it received the slightest hint of an answer, never once in all the ages the least suggestion of an answer—aside from God. And, depend on it, if Jesus, son of man and Son of God, had never come into the world, that sad question would have echoed around the world, up and down the corridors of all the centuries, unanswered and unanswerable until this very day.

"O Plato!" cried Socrates, "it may be that the gods can forgive sins, but alas! I do not see how!" No. Nor can anyone else! Job's question fell back upon his face. The universe could give him no reply. Philosophy could find no reply. Nature could give him no reply. Only God.

"I have sinned—what shall I do?" "I have sinned!" Pharaoh said it. "I have sinned!" Balaam said it. "I have sinned!" King Saul said it. "I have sinned!" Achan said it. "I have sinned!" David said it. "I have sinned!" Judas said it. "I have sinned!" The prodigal said it. "I have sinned!" Millions, in chorus of confirmation, have said it. "I have sinned!" Millions are saying it now. "I have sinned!" *I* have said it. *You* have said it. *All* of us have said it.

"I have sinned!" What shall I do? We may scour sea and land for some answer to that sad question of the soul. We may search earth and sky for some answer to that wild question of the soul. We may climb the lofty summits of the mountains seeking to find some answer to that question. We may thread the labyrinthine mine, hoping to find some answer to that question. We may call to the heights of the heavens. We may call to the depths of the sea. But there will be no answering voice. And we are left to nurse a piteous despair until we come to—

> . . . a green hill far away,
> Without a city wall,
> Where our dear Lord was crucified,
> Who died to save us all!

No man knows of any other fount in all the wide universe of God, which has cleansing efficacy for sin, except the fountain which was opened in the riven side of our Lord Jesus, our Redeemer—that fountain "filled with blood drawn from Immanuel's veins"—that fountain

beneath which sinners are plunged and "lose all their
guilty stains." That is the only sufficient and efficient
fountain for sin and uncleanness. Where else can men
discharge that crimson stain of sin? Nowhere else. Can
the pool of Siloam do it? No. Can the snows of Hermon
wash us whiter than snow? No. Has the Jordan in full
spate power to cleanse us from the foulness of our human
guilt? No. Can Abanar and Pharpar, rivers of Damascus,
rid us of our leprosy? Can all the multitudinous seas
wash us and make us clean? No. Never.

> None other Lamb, none other Name,
>   None other hope in heaven or earth or sea;
> None other hiding place from guilt and shame,
>   None beside Thee!

There is no other hiding place. The refuge of morality
is roofless and wall-less. Man has a veil for armor when
he wraps the righteous robe of his respectability about
him. Man has a roofless ruin for a house when he trusts
in his self-righteousness—thanking God in his pharisaic
complacency that he is not as other men are, "extor-
tioners, thieves, adulterers, unjust," or "even as this
publican." A man finds any fence of ethical superiority
in which he attempts to enclose himself to be a very
flimsy refuge. A refuge of lies will go down in ruin with
one blast of the terrible One. All life aside from life in
Jesus Christ is stormy. Other refuge have we none!

In the day of accusation, when conscience rises as a
strong armed man, we shall need a defense far more
substantial than a man-made refuge. In this day of dis-
crimination when God makes searching inquisition for
sin, all our fine-spun philosophies will prove to be of no
avail. When the foundations of the earth are being removed, the heavens roll up as a scroll, the firmament
melts in the heat of the final conflagration, and the
judgment flames lick all the waterways into paths of

dust, we shall come to that eternal refuge, the Rock of Ages.

> Rock of Ages, cleft for me,
> Let me hide myself in Thee;
> Let the water and the blood,
> From Thy wounded side which flowed,
> Be of sin the double cure,
> Save from wrath and make me pure.
>
> Could my tears forever flow,
> Could my zeal no languor know,
> These for sin could not atone;
> Thou must save, and Thou alone:
> In my hand no price I bring,
> Simply to Thy cross I cling.
>
> While I draw this fleeting breath,
> When my eyes shall close in death,
> When I rise to worlds unknown,
> And behind Thee on Thy throne,
> Rock of Ages, cleft for me,
> Let me hide myself in Thee.

The question, "What shall I do with my sins?" God answers out of the whirlwind of man's remorse.

The question, "If a man die, shall he live again?" God answers out of the storm of human sorrow. He answers it by giving a divine hope to the travail of the ages. By the empty tomb in Joseph's garden, He gives a note of gladness to a world of sorrow, a note of hope to a world of despair, a note of assurance to a world of doubt, a note of victory to a world of defeat. In many ways, but chiefly through Jesus Christ who hath brought life and immortality to light through the Gospel (II Timothy 1:10), He answers that question. The eternal God, who answered Job out of the whirlwind, is not baffled by any question that man lays before Him. Our most profound questions are not puzzles to Him. God, the eternal God, who hath His way in the whirlwind, is not perplexed by our perplexities. God, whose whirlwind

goeth forth with fury, a *continuing* whirlwind, is not
baffled by what baffles us, is not wearied by what
wearies us, is not discouraged by what discourages us,
is not mystified by what mystifies us. "God answered
Job out of the whirlwind!" God has an answer for all
our questions, pains, and cares through Christ His
greatest revelation who Himself once asked, in painful
soul suffering, "Why hast thou forsaken me?"

III. The Whirlwinds of God Speak of the Harvest Day

For they have sown the wind, and they shall reap the whirlwind
(Hosea 8:7).

These are the words Hosea used in speaking of how
destruction would come upon the house of the Lord for
impiety and idolatry. Hosea summed up the punishment
that would come to them because of their numerous
transgressions in one sentence, saying, "They have
sown the wind, and they shall reap the whirlwind."

Life is a mystery. Death is a mystery. Men often ponder life and death. God has never revealed life and death
to us. The mystery is known to God alone.

Growth is another mystery that only God understands.
Deeply impressed by the fact and the mystery of growth,
we have marveled at the principle that controls the harvest.

Whatsoever a man soweth, that shall he also reap for he that
soweth to his flesh shall of the flesh reap corruption; but he that
soweth to the Spirit shall of the Spirit reap life everlasting (Galatians 6:8).

In other words, like produces like. He who sows wheat
reaps wheat, not pepper. He who plants a grape reaps a
purple cluster, not a bunch of thorns or a sprig of this-
tles. He who sows honor, reaps confidence and honor. He
who plants figs gathers figs, not berries. He who sows

grass, reaps grass, not moss. He who plants cotton, gathers cotton, not pumpkins. Nature's law, all men know, is universal and inexorable—like produces like. The sheaf is simply the seed enlarged. The bale of cotton is simply the seed enlarged and multiplied through the mystery of growth. The sowing contains the germ of all harvests to be reaped.

If a man sows the wind, he shall reap the whirlwind. If a home sows the wind, it shall reap the whirlwind. If a nation sows the wind, it shall reap the whirlwind. If a woman sows the wind, she shall reap the whirlwind. That has been true in all the years that are buried forever in the tomb of time. That will be true of all the years that may come from the womb of time. If a man sows the wind, he will reap the whirlwind. If a man sows tares, he will reap tares. It may not be today. It may not be to-morrow. It may not be this week. It may not be next week. It may not be this year. It may not be next year. But the time of reaping will surely come—just as surely as night follows day. When the reaping time comes, the harvest will be sad. Those who have sown bad seed and reaped a bad harvest will offer to exchange places with the Christians whom they despised, shunned, and believed to be foolish.

When the whirlwind harvest day comes, I do not think the murderous Cain would need an argument to get him to exchange places with the spiritual Abel. No cowardly Pilate would need persuasion to induce him to exchange places with Elijah, the prophet of God, or with Obadiah "who feared the Lord in Ahab's house." If John the Baptist's place were offered him, Herod would quickly accept it. If she had the opportunity, Jezebel would gladly take Dorcas' place. A delegation would not be necessary to go to Nero to argue with him to get to exchange places with Paul. A man would not have to use eloquent words to persuade Potiphar's wife to exchange places with Joseph. There would be no delay on Dives' part in accepting Lazarus' place if it were offered him. In his last moments Clarence Darrow would probably have given all that he had to be able to die like William Jennings Bryan. It was Mr. Moody who, in his Spirit-led way, often repeated the truth that though the worldling may look with contempt upon Christians, the time is coming when the worldling will give anything to exchange places with the meanest Christian that walks the streets.

Never doubt the truth that those who sow the wind will reap the whirlwind. Do not doubt this truth even though the harvest is slow, though it comes on leaden heels. Notice this passage from God's eternal Book:

> Because sentence against an evil work is not executed speedily, therefore the heart of the sons of men is fully set in them to do evil.
> Though a sinner do evil a hundred times, and his days be prolonged, yet surely I know that it shall be well with them that fear God, which fear before him: but it shall not be well with the wicked, neither shall he prolong his days, which are as a shadow; because he feareth not before God (Ecclesiastes 8:11-13).

Years ago, years too far gone for some of us to remember well, a man and a woman killed their illegitimately born child. Years went by. But the harvest day came, though it seemed to come slowly. The day of the whirlwind came—the terrible harvest day, when their deeds came back upon them, when they gathered the sheaves of their sowing. They had gone out to the far Northwest. The man was found frozen one day, standing upright in a huge snowdrift, where the blizzard had overtaken them. At his back gaped the portal of a mountain gorge, a wintry chaos of glacier-riven rock and snow-laden firs. The woman was found in a sheltered corner in the gorge. The ice king had breathed on her too. The woman was crouched before the ashes of an extinct fire. Around her lay the widely scattered contents of a treasure box which

held all their belongings. Clutched close to her breast,
as though she would shield it from storm, lay a strange
bundle—a faded shawl rolled into the semblance of the
form of a child. Written with blackened ember on the
frozen whiteness of the icy wall behind her were these
words, "The Wages of Sin is Death." They sowed the
wind. They reaped the whirlwind.

There are a great many things in this world of which
we are not sure. We are not sure we shall reach the end
of the voyage we start at the wharf, or the end of a railroad journey we start at the depot. We are not sure we
will finish the book we begin to read. We are not sure we
will plow to the end of the furrow in the field. We are not
sure when we go to sleep that we shall wake again in this
world. We are not sure when we greet the sunrise that we
shall be here to greet the sunset. But there is one thing
we are sure of, all nations are sure of, all peoples are
sure of, and every individual is sure of, for God has said
it: "Whatsoever a man soweth, that shall he also reap."

"They have sown the wind, and they shall reap the
whirlwind." There is not a "probably" attached to that
statement. There is no "perhaps" before or behind it.
There is no uncertainty dwelling in it. There is no "may-
be-so" found in it anywhere. The idea of uncertainty is
nowhere to be found in it. "They that have sown the wind
shall reap the whirlwind." What harvest awaits you?

> Sowing the seed by the daylight fair,
> Sowing the seed by the noonday glare,
> Sowing the seed by the fading light,
> Sowing the seed in the solemn night;
> Oh, what shall the harvest be?
> Oh, what shall the harvest be?
>
> Sowing the seed by the wayside high,
> Sowing the seed on the rocks to die,
> Sowing the seed where the thorns will spoil,

Sowing the seed in the fertile soil;
Oh, what shall the harvest be?
Oh, what shall the harvest be?

Sowing the seed of a lingering pain,
Sowing the seed of a maddened brain,
Sowing the seed of a tarnished name,
Sowing the seed of eternal shame;
Oh, what shall the harvest be?
Oh, what shall the harvest be?

Sowing the seed of an aching heart,
Sowing the seed while the teardrops start,
Sowing in hope till the reapers come,
Gladly to gather the harvest home;
Oh, what shall the harvest be?
Oh, what shall the harvest be?

IV. THE WHIRLWINDS OF GOD SPEAK OF RETRIBUTION

Because I have called, and ye refused; I have stretched out my hand, and no man regarded; but ye have set at naught all my council, and would none of my reproof: I also laugh at your calamity; I will mock when your fear cometh; when your fear cometh as desolation, and your destruction cometh as a whirlwind; when distress and anguish cometh upon you. Then shall they call upon me, but I will not answer; they shall seek me early, but they shall not find me (Proverbs 1:24-28).

"I will laugh . . . I will mock . . . when your destruction cometh *as a whirlwind!*" This is no philosophical aphorism. This is no empty threatening. This is no catchy quip. This is no linguistic twist of words. This is no limerick of levity. It is the language of divine inspiration—language clothed with the eternal truth of Him who cannot lie, and backed by the arm of inexorable justice, which will sooner or later verify it. Apply it where you will. Apply it to the churches. Apply it to the minister. Apply it to the sinner reveling in his midnight debaucheries.

Apply it to the woman who hires herself out as a harlot. Apply it to the man who holds woman's virtue of little worth. Apply it to the nations that have forgotten God. Apply it to the man who makes money without regard for man or God. Wherever there is sin collectively or individually, it has a retribution day, a day of finding out the sinner.

Knowing this, know also that it is dangerous to do wrong. Sin's road may seem to be soft and smooth, but sin's road grows rough toward the end, and ends in black night. Sin plants its flowers and puts underneath each one of them a tarantula. Sin spreads its silken and downy couch of indulgence which outwardly appears beautiful, but has a nest of brooding serpents underneath it. Sin opens sparkling pleasure fountains, but every one who drinks from them drinks water which is more bitter than the bitter waters of Marah. Sin, with opaline lights, lures us out to sea, and then, in the horror of the night, strangles our cry in the deep. Sin promises us substance and store if we will walk its deceptive streets, and then, having pierced our feet with thorns, it leaves us to stumble on to the dungeons of hell.

The stag pursued by hungry hounds is not more miserable than the man who is pursued by his sins. The bird taken in the fowler's net laboring vainly to escape is less wretched than the woman who, yielding to sin's enticement, has woven about herself a web of deception. An eagle, once used to the sunlight heights, but now beating his wings out against the brass bars of his cage, is less unhappy than the man who has a skeleton in his house of life. A swimmer in storm-stirred sea, harassed by the sight of a shark's jaws near by, is not more tormented than the man who goes on to meet the retributive hour of his sinning. The fish in the talons of a hawk has more comfort than the man whose conscience scourges him down life's road to meet his just retribution. The serpent

writhing and hissing in a bed of hot coals is not to be
pitied more than the man or woman who has come to
sin's retributive payday. The judge may seem to be un-
observant. The watchman may seem to be asleep. But
God never slumbers. Law never sleeps.

A recent newspaper article told of a Negro man in
Arkansas who had a pet rattlesnake. The Negro found
the snake when it was very young. He took it, fed it and
made quite a pet of it. The reptile would come when he
whistled. It would eat from his fingers. It would coil
around his arm and let him stroke its head with the palm
of his hand or with the tips of his fingers. One day he
took it to town to exhibit it among his friends. They
marveled at its gentleness, the way it coiled itself with
apparent gentleness around his arm, how it would come
when he whistled, and that it would eat from his hand.
He went home with his pet. Suddenly, with only the
slightest provocation, the reptile became angry. Quicker
than the zig-zag lightning flashes from the bosom of a
dark cloud, the pet rattler buried its fangs in the black
man's arm. The poisonous fangs of the serpent brought
death in one quick instant. Two nights later, the man who
should have been sitting with his family in their humble
but happy home was sleeping in the mud of an Arkansas
grave. This is the ill fate of every man and woman who
makes a pet of sin. Horror and death come to every
man who refuses to hear God's call. An hour of like
terror awaits the man or woman who does not respond to
God's outstretched arm. Dread despair like the negro
experienced when he pulled the pet snake's fangs from
his arm and hurled it to the ground, is yet to be en-
countered by all who set God's counsel at naught and will
have none of his reproof. "Be not deceived; God is not
mocked." Turn at God's reproof. Turn now. There's
danger and death in delay. Let that sin go. Drop it—now.

Dr Lee Rutland Scarborough, burden-bearer for God,

told me of having received a message fraught with sadness and woe.

"Mr. So-and-So has shot himself and he is calling for you!"

The man of God, ready and willing to help, was soon by the man's side. It was a home of poverty, neglect, and sin. The man had been on a drunken spree for two weeks. Recovering from the wild time, he found himself sick and discouraged. He took his own pistol and shot himself. This is what Dr. L. R. Scarborough said,

"He took my hand at seven in the morning, and I was not able to get free from his grip until eleven, when his hand fell pulseless at his side. I begged him for hours to give his heart to Christ. Just before he died I called his family. His oldest boy, fourteen years of age, hugged and kissed his father goodbye. I will never forget what that father said to that son. The children came one after another until the sixth one, the baby, came. Finally, he said goodbye to his wife who was a Christian woman. He took her by the hand, still holding on to mine.

" 'Molly,' he said, 'you have been a good wife. These sixteen years you did all the praying. You studied the Bible and taught the Word of God to our children. You went to church and lived a godly life. I have not helped you at all, Molly. For sixteen years you have stood for me in religion. Now, I am dying and I want to know if you are going to stand for me at the judgment bar of God.

"The pale woman with tear stained face turned to me for an answer. I said, 'Old fellow, your faithful wife has done everything she could for you, but at the judgment bar of God you will have to stand in your own shoes.'

"He died—and went out to meet God unprepared."

Retribution! Destruction coming as the whirlwind. There is a question *I* cannot answer. There is a question *you* cannot answer. There is a question which *all the knowledge of all the scholars* of the world cannot answer. There is a question all our *scientists* cannot answer. A question the *angels* cannot answer. A question all the *intelligences in earth and heaven* cannot answer. A question *God* in heaven cannot answer. The question is: How can we escape if we neglect the salvation which delivers us from sin's dread penalty? How, if men keep on sinning, refusing when God calls, regarding not when God stretches out his hand—how can they escape the dread day of retribution when God will laugh at their calamity, when He will mock their desolation? If men keep on in sin's road, their fear will come as desolation and their destruction will come as a whirlwind.

V. THE WHIRLWINDS OF GOD SPEAK OF THE HOUR OF FAREWELL

And it came to pass, when the Lord would take up Elijah into heaven by a whirlwind, that Elijah went with Elisha from Gilgal. And Elijah said unto Elisha, Tarry here, I pray thee; for the Lord hath sent me to Bethel. And Elisha said unto him, As the Lord liveth, and as thy soul liveth, I will not leave thee. So they went down to Bethel. And the sons of the prophets that were at Bethel came forth to Elisha, and said unto him, Knowest thou that the Lord will take away thy master from thy head today? And he said, Yea, I know it; hold ye your peace. And Elijah said unto him, Elisha, tarry here, I pray thee; for the Lord hath sent me to Jericho. And he said, As the Lord liveth, and as thy soul liveth, I will not leave thee. So they came to Jericho. And the sons of the prophets that were at Jericho came to Elisha, and said unto him, Knowest thou that the Lord will take away thy master from thy head today? And he answered, Yea, I know it; hold ye your peace. And Elijah said unto him, Tarry, I pray thee, here; for the Lord hath sent me to Jordan. And he said, As the Lord liveth, and as thy soul liveth, I will not leave thee. And they two went on. And fifty men of the sons of the prophets went, and stood to view afar off: and they two stood by Jordan. And Elijah took his mantle, and wrapped it together, and smote the waters, and they were divided hither and thither, so that they two went over on dry ground. And it came to pass, when they were gone over, that Elijah said unto Elisha, Ask what I shall do for thee, before I be taken away from thee. And Elisha said, I pray thee, let a double portion of thy spirit be upon me. And he said, Thou hast asked a hard thing: nevertheless, if thou see me when I am taken from thee, it shall be so unto thee; but if not, it shall not be so. And it came to pass, as they still went on, and talked, that, behold, there appeared a chariot of fire, and horses of fire, and parted them both asunder; **and Elijah went up by a whirlwind into heaven** (II Kings 2:1-11).

" . . . up by a whirlwind!" It was goodbye. Here is a lesson for us. It is this; there is a time of going for us. Another lesson; the time of our going is in the Lord's hands, and the way of our going is of the Lord's determination. One says, "I want to go on my birthday." But God wills that it shall not be so. One says, "I want to die a lingering death." But God says, "No, suddenly thou shalt go. Suddenly a bolt shall strike thee. Thou shalt go to bed well, and with the morning shalt be in heaven —without a pain, a spasm, or notice given to any one!" Another says, "I want to go with my friends around me, their hands holding mine, their ears hearing my last voice." But God may will it that thou shalt die in loneliness—away from friends, among strangers. Another says, "I should like to go as a shock of corn fully ripe." But God may will that thou shalt be cut down in the greenness of thy youth! All of which is to say that the farewells concerning which the whirlwinds that took up Elijah speak are realities awaiting us across a near-by Jordan, across a far-away Jordan.

Goodbye—separation—some day. God's whirlwind speaks of this.

Goodbye—separation—the ships sailing from the harbor say so.

Goodbye—separation—the trains, massive juggernauts of steel and steam, puffing out of terminal stations and away from village depots and speeding across the lands, say so.

Goodbye—separation—the airplanes, arousing the lands with roaring noise, and mounting on steel wings to the eagle's domain and swooping across continents and seas, say so.

Goodbye—separation—to this the automobiles testify as they speed over our highways, seen and gone in a moment.

Goodbye—separation—to this the loud voice of Mars testifies as he walks with bloody boots across the gardens of the world, with bloody fingers tying crepe on the door knob of millions of homes.

Goodbye—separation—in the court room when a mother, struggling like a Spartan to keep the tears, says "Goodbye" to her boy being taken to prison—or to the death house.

Goodbye—separation—of this mother kissing her child as it goes off to school for the first time.

Goodbye—separation—this is the reality that shadows the heart of the mother sitting with a dead baby in her lap.

Goodbye—separation—this is the inevitable result as the bride, with the one upon whom her love has been fastened, leaves the old home nest.

Goodbye—separation—in childhood. In youth. In old age. All the time. Among all peoples. Everywhere!

"Parted . . . asunder" (II Kings 2:11).

"And Eliska . . . saw him no more" (II Kings 2:12).

Yes, that is the way it is. "Parted asunder!" We all know what that means.

"And Elisha saw him no more!" We all know what that means.

Mothers taken away from little children, and the children see them no more—parted asunder.

Fathers taken from the household, and the families see them no more. Parted asunder.

Husbands taken from the arms of wives, and the wives see them no more. Parted asunder.

Sons marching to war, choosing the garments of flame and blood as their garments of glory, parted asunder from loved ones who see them no more. Parted asunder.

Little children, whose laughter was the sweetest music of the household, whose smiles made sunshine for the home, taken from the arms of mothers, and mothers, longing for them, see them no more. Parted asunder.

Youth turning from the old home gate to seek his fortune in the great city, leaving the old homestead, and he sees the old home no more. Oft 'tis so. Parted asunder.

Multitudes in the city and multitudes in the country scattering flowers on tomb-marked graves. Multitudes down by desolate seashores that reach in ragged lines around the world scattering flowers on the ocean, which is a tomb of tombs, a vast mausoleum, hoping, with the blue light of the ageless morning, to see those from whom they are parted. Here we learn that the pain of love is parting.

Youth comes and is parted from childhood. We see our childhood no more. Old age, insidious and lethal, comes before we want it and before we realize it. We are parted from our youth—we see it no more.

The money for which we toiled is lost in the bank crash or in some foolish investment. Parted from our money, we see it no more.

Fame comes and crowns us with a withering crown. Then, by some misstep or by the brighter shining of the crown of one who has outdone us, fame leaves. Parted from the feeble candles of fame which are blown out by the same crowd that applauded us, we see fame no more.

The accumulation of property comes, but, before we know it, the time comes to go and leave it to the hands of another. All we then require is a small area about six feet long and two feet wide—the same a beggar requires. Parted from our accumulations we take none of them with us.

But why continue in this strain? "Parted . . . asunder!" "And Elisha . . . saw him no more." These words put before us experiences familiar to every one of us—experiences our forefathers in the dim past knew about, experiences we ourselves are familiar with, experiences which our children's children shall understand. But what does it matter—all this parting asunder as when Elijah went up by a whirlwind into heaven—if for a little while we do *not* see them, and in a little while we *shall* see them? What victory hath this parting with our accumulations if our going is but to see treasures we laid up in heaven? What sadness hath our being parted from our loved ones if it is to greet redeemed loved ones in the other world? What sting hath our going if it is God's whirlwind that comes for us? What sorrow is in our staying behind when others go—if we have the Lord God of Elijah with us? What sadness is there in walking alone—if, at our word, the Lord God will part the waters of Jordan? Why bitter tears when one of God's days we shall be with our loved ones forever—if God sent for them to be with him? Darling baby of the heart, I shall have you and love you forever. Think of that—when the chariot and the whirlwind goeth up. Mother, you whose going up was like a soldier from warfare, I shall love you and have you forever. Father, you whose leaving was, to you, like a sailor home from a stormy sea, I shall have you forever. Friend of mine, you whose leaving stopped the singing of the birds, I shall have you forever. Lover, you whose going plucked the sun out of life's sky, I shall have you forever. Comrade, comrade, you who denied my heart's yearning to stay a little longer, I shall have you forever. The chariot shall come for me, even as it came for you.

And, in this belief, we shall face the farewell of our friends and the goodbye from our loved ones in the spirit of Elijah as he went from Gilgal with Elisha, as he came to Bethel with Elisha, as he came to Jericho with Elisha, as he crossed over Jordan with Elisha in calmness and dignity and unspeakable tenderness.

As it was with Elijah when the whirlwind from heaven brought him home, so shall our farewells here be changed into greetings yonder. And we, as Stanton standing in the shadows sang, can say:

> Adieu, sweet friends—I have waited long
>   To hear the message that calls me home,
> And now it comes like a low sweet song
>   Of welcome over the river's foam;
> And my heart shall ache and my feet shall roam
>   No more—no more: I am going home!
>
> Home! where no storm—where no tempest raves,
>   In the light of the calm, eternal day;
> Where no willows weep over lonely graves
>   And the tears from our eyelids are kissed away.
> And my soul shall sigh, and my feet shall roam
>   No more—no more: I am going home!

CHAPTER 2

THE PATHS OF DISAPPOINTMENT

Vanity of vanities; all is vanity (Ecclesiates 1:2).

The word "vanity" occurs thirty-seven times in the book of Ecclesiastes. Moreover, vanity is the key-word of the book of Ecclesiastes—the keynote to its dirgelike message.

"Vanity of vanities! All is vanity!" These words are not due to a fit of temporary depression. They are not given utterance because of some passing adverse circumstance. They were not born of the quick and passing bitterness begotten by the foul play of some friend who turned traitor. Subtle pride did not prompt this language of Solomon. They are, according to our judgment, the result of experience arrived at after mature and deliberate thought.

They are not the words of a man who walked a *few* paths, but the words of a man who walked *many* paths. Not the words of one whose "little body was aweary of this big world." Nor the words of one bored with the routine of some prosaic task. Nor the words of a man whose courage failed in some steep ascent of toil. Nor the words of one in prostrate rebellion against the tortures of some couch of pain.

These are the words of one who sailed over many seas of human experience and made special notes and charts of his voyages with deliberate care. They are words of

32

one who drank of every cup and wrote a label for each. They are words of a man who explored every house and wrote wisdom upon the walls for those who enter to ponder, and placarded the outside for all who pass to read. And in these words Solomon, Solomon the wise, Solomon the rich, Solomon the mighty, has left the testimony that even a king could not find and cannot find genuine satisfaction in things finite, in things perishing, in things of the earth—earthy!

By what path shall I go to find the home of perfect happiness? Which road must I take to compass heart satisfaction? What must I do to find contentment? What —to have a "good time"? What—to be superior to the habitations in which I am domiciled? What—to have a merry heart within the stern war of things? What—to have a mouth filled with laughter in bitter strife? What— to be anchored in peace in the swift current of facts? What—to know the intoxication of pleasure without dissipation of the soul's finest resources? What—to fill the years and yet avoid evacuations of the heart's abiding places?

In answer, Solomon tried out five paths—discarding each in turn, until he cried over the grave of all disappointed hopes, as his life's fair morning died in dark sunset, "Vanity of vanities; all is vanity!" These five paths, which he tried and traveled and found to be paths of disappointment, men try and travel today. And these five paths are the only paths which men try. These five paths, girt oft with flowers, crowded oft with sojourners, beset oft with pits, compass all the experiences and imaginations of men. Let us be content to give these five paths telescopic observation, for we shall not have time to give them microscopic scrutiny. May the instruction thereof be received. May the warning therein be heeded.

Observe first:

I. The Path of Wisdom

I gave my heart to know wisdom, and to know madness and folly
(Ecclesiastes 1:17).

Solomon knew everything as nearly as mortal man
could know everything. His was no capsule brain cap-
able only of tidbits. He was a scientist. He was a philosopher. He was a moralist and a historian. He was a
publicist and a poet. He had a mind trained to observe
—to meditate. He had an imagination by which he interpreted the facts of history and built upon the premise
of these facts the deductions of science. He walked
familiarly through the fields of botany. "He spake of
trees, from the cedar tree that is in Lebanon even unto
the hyssop that springeth out of the wall" (1 Kings
4:33). He brought forth the treasures of the mine. He
knew nature's choir made up of the voices of birds, wind
in the boughs, and the seashore. He interpreted the messages of the heavenly bodies. He sailed the seas. He knew
the birds. He wrote parables from the fields and the
forests. He gathered great wealth of gold and precious
stones. He wrote and published books. He wrote thousands of imperishable proverbs. He interpreted human
experience. He philosophized about divine revelation.

But, with all this, he missed the one essential and
found no rest for his heart. It is he, this great Solomon
with all his glory, who, after roaming through all the
realms of thought and imagination, of human wisdom
and human knowledge, cried "Vanity of vanities; all is
vanity!"

"And I gave my heart to know wisdom, and to know
madness and folly: I perceived that this also is vexation
of spirit" (Ecclesiastes 1:17).

Once, as a great servant of the Lord tells us, a man
traveled a long way—a journey of many miles—to in-
terview a distinguished scholar. The butler ushered him

in, upon the presentation of his card, into the study of the great scholar. He was cordially greeted. Before seating himself he asked this question of the noted scholar,

"Doctor, I have come a long way to ask you one question. I observe that the walls of your room are filled with books. This room is literally lined with them from ceiling to floor. I suppose you have read them all. I know you have written many books. You have traveled the world over; you have held intimate converse with the world's wisest men—its leaders of thought, its creators of opinion. Tell me, if you will, after the years you have spent in study, out of the things you have learned, what is the *one* thing best worth knowing?"

The great scholar's face flushed with emotion. He placed, with clumsy gentleness, both hands over the hands of his caller. And he said,

"My dear sir, out of all the things I have learned there are two lessons worth knowing. The first is, I am a great sinner. The second is, Jesus Christ is a great Saviour. In the knowledge of these two facts as applied in my own personal experiences lies all my happiness and all my hope!"

Thus we learn, from that man's answer, that men may know some things and not the best things—the things most worth knowing. Thus we see that men may treasure rags and throw away treasures. Yes, though many may not see it, a man may know all about the rocks, and his heart may be hard as they. A man may know all about the winds, and his life be swept by passions fiercer than they. A man may know all about the tides and the seas, and his life resemble their troubled waters that rest not and know no peace. A man may know all about lights— the light of showers of meteors, the light of phosphorus, the light of millions of stars, the light of the moon when it hangs like a sickle, candle light, lamp light, electric light, the light of the aurora borealis—and not know Jesus who said "I am the light of the world." A man may know all about the roads in the country, roads in the jungle, roads through burning deserts, and not know Jesus who said, "I am the way."

All of which brings us to say—to ask—what shall it profit a man IF? If—in questions that use another's words.

What shall it profit a man if he be a great artist and know not Jesus, the One Altogether Lovely?

What shall it profit a man if he be a great architect and know not Jesus, the Chief Corner Stone?

What shall it profit a man if he be a great baker and know not Jesus, the Living Bread?

What shall it profit a man if he be a great banker and know not Jesus, the Priceless Possession?

What shall it profit a man if he be a great biologist and know not Jesus, the Life?

What shall it profit a man if he be a great builder and know not Jesus, the Sure Foundation?

What shall it profit a man if he be a great carpenter and know not Jesus, the Door?

What shall it profit a man if he be a great doctor and know not Jesus, the Great Physician?

What shall it profit a man if he be a great educator and know not Jesus, the Teacher?

What shall it profit a man if he be a great engineer and know not Jesus, the New and Living Way?

What shall it profit a man if he be a great farmer and know not Jesus, the Sower and Lord of Harvests?

What shall it profit a man if he be a great florist and know not Jesus, the Rose of Sharon?

What shall it profit a man if he be a great geologist and know not Jesus, the Rock of Ages?

What shall it profit a man if he be a great astronomer and know not Jesus, the Star of Bethlehem?

What shall it profit a man if he be a great horticulturist and know not Jesus, the True Vine?

What shall it profit a man if he be a great judge and know not Jesus, the Righteous Judge?

What shall it profit a man if he be a great jurist and know not Jesus, the True Witness?

What shall it profit a man if he be a great jeweler and know not Jesus, the Pearl of Great Price?

What shall it profit a man if he be a great lawyer and know not Jesus, the Sinner's Advocate?

What shall it profit a man if he be a great philanthropist and know not Jesus, the Unspeakable Gift?

What shall it profit a man if he be a great philosopher and know not Jesus, the Wisdom of God?

What shall it profit a man if he be a great sculptor and know not Jesus, the Living Stone?

What shall it profit a man if he be a great student and know not Jesus, the Incarnate Truth?

What shall it profit a man if he be a great sinner and know not Jesus, the Lamb of God?

"And I gave my heart to know wisdom, and to know madness and folly. I perceived that this also is vanity and vexation of spirit" (Ecclesiates 1:17).

That is something of what Paul, the great apostle meant when he wrote:

"And though I have the gift of prophecy, and understand all mysteries, and all knowledge; and though I have all faith, so that I could remove mountains, and have not charity, I am nothing (I Cor. 13:2).

Mere human wisdom never satisfies. Call this world wee, or call it great. Even if we knew all things, there are many things we never would and never could know. Millions of things we do not know. Write down all we know—it will be a small volume. Write down all we do not know of things in the heavens and things in the earth and things under the earth, it would be a large

library of many shelves and many large volumes. But
even if we knew all that there is to know of human
knowledge, it would be a path of disappointment if,
in knowing so much, we did not learn the two things
most worth knowing.

Man, in the course of his life, lays down one world
after another. First, the infant's world of toys is abandoned. Second, the boy's world of games, amusements.
So also the youth's world of schemes, enterprises, the
dreams of progress and wealth. The path of disappointment is the path of human wisdom that excludes the
things best worth knowing and most worth knowing.

Solomon sought experience and found disappointment
in

II. THE PATH OF WINE

I sought in mine heart, to give myself unto wine, yet acquainting
mine heart with wisdom; . . . till I might see what was that good
for the sons of men, which they should do under the heaven all the
days of their life (Ecclesiastes 2:3).

Having tried the path of earthly knowledge and wisdom, and failing to find guest room in the house of
happiness, Solomon next turns to wine. "Wine that
maketh glad the heart" (Psalm 104:15). And so we hear
him saying, "Come, now, I will prove thee with mirth,
therefore enjoy thou pleasure"—that is, the pleasure
wine is supposed to give. So Solomon "descends to the
realm of the purely physical to cheer his flesh with wine."
I do not think he "descended to the low plain of sordid
drunkenness," for he said, "I . . . give myself to wine, *yet
acquainting my heart with wisdom.*" Doubtless Solomon
was not in the gutter. Doubtless he never did some of
the fool things men do when they are under the influence
of wine. But it was he who wrote:

Who hath woe? who hath sorrow? who hath contentions? who
hath babbling? who hath wounds without cause? who hath redness

of eyes? They that tarry long at the wine; they that go to seek mixed wine. Look not thou upon the wine when it is red, when it giveth his color in the cup, when it moveth itself aright. At the last it biteth like a serpent, and stingeth like an adder. Thine eyes shall behold strange women, and thine heart shall utter perverse things. Yea, thou shalt be as he that lieth down in the midst of the sea, or as he that lieth upon the top of the mast. They have stricken me, shalt thou say, and I was not sick; they have beaten me, and I felt it not: when shall I awake? I will seek it yet again (Prov. 23:29-35).

He discovered for himself and transmitted to future generations the bitterness of that experience and observation which finds in the dregs of the sparkling cup, the sting of the adder, the poison of the serpent! Solomon, while doubtless never a debased drunkard, "learned the ropes" of the wine realm. The warnings he has given against the bottle are vivid and true.

The follies of the wine realm are still with us. The bitter fruit of the wine press is with us. The sins of the wine cup are rampant. There is the wine domination of certain social circles. There is the wine domination of certain customs. "There is the wine iniquity of certain political institutions, parties, and governments. Perhaps no factor in American life has dealt with a more arrogant hand. Perhaps no factor in our American life has carried a mightier weight of influence in social, commercial, political life than the wine business—the iniquitous whiskey business, the business without a conscience, the business without a care for the welfare of others."

But I am not to speak of the drink business as a national curse, but as an individual curse, blight, and enormous sin. With many, what is the high mark of sociability today? The offer and the acceptance of the invitation to "have a drink!" The drink involved in this invitation, however, is not *water*—water never once. Always *strong* drink. I have never understood why a man should be understood as having consideration for my welfare when he offers me that which dims my eyes, dulls my senses, ties up my tongue, addles my brain, and blights my life. And I have never understood why a man should not invite me, or why he should take offense if I should invite him, to have a social drink of castor oil or milk of magnesia. It does not taste much worse than liquor, and it would have a far more remedial effect. But it is just not done in society. To "have a drink," whether it is at the club-house, the business office, the hotel room, the college hop or on the joy ride is to drink liquor— some form of alcoholic beverage. Does it bring joy? No, every drop is loaded with disappointment.

The college student who carries "hooch on the hip" knows it will hurt his health and bring him disappointment. The foolish young woman who takes delight in "taking a nip" from some sheik's flask knows that it will harm her physically and mentally. There is as much tragedy as fun in the statement

> Jack and Jill
> Went up the hill
> To get some bootleg liquor;
> Jack went blind
> And lost his mind,
> And Jill is even sicker!

Five drunk men, after the midnight hour had passed, leaned against a telephone post in front of Mrs. Smith's home, knowing not whence they came nor whither they went. They shouted and whooped and hiccoughed. The lady of the house, angry beyond words, threw open the window. She angrily shouted, "Hello!" One of the drunks, with a wave of his hand and a bob of his head, said belchingly, "Hello, you, there—you Mrs. Smith?"

"Yes," came the sharp, snapping answer. "What do you want?"

"Please, ma'am, you," hic-ingly and with another

wave of the hand and other bobs of the head, "Lady, won't you, lady, come out and pick out Mr. Smith so the rest of us fellows can go home?"

Men have done more foolish and far more tragic things than that under the influence of strong drink. Some, under its demoniac spell, have gone home at night not knowing a buzz saw from a silver dollar, thinking the keyhole the entrance to Mammoth Cave,—and the clothes wire a railroad track. Some, mastered by the demon of drink, have gone their way with murder in their eyes and hands. This is an old story—and a modern story. A huge bottle would be an appropriate tombstone over many graves. Certainly a bottle in reality, whether visible or not, is the tombstone that stands above ruined hopes, broken families, disappointments, bitterness, and all misery. The bottle, the cup, the weak will, the blasted career—then the grave with a bottle as a tombstone. That is the story.

Hooch, hell-raising hooch, is, with many, a word with which to charm. Tarrying long at the wine is the chief indoor sport of those who seek to cheer their flesh at the expense of their health and at the higher expense of their souls.

But all who have walked the wine path, whether they be old, or young, have found that "wine is a mocker, strong drink is raging, and whosoever is deceived thereby is not wise" (Prov. 20:1). This is not only the truth of God, but it is the verdict of the ages. Let us consider that verdict—as given us recently in words of wisdom.

On an early Egyptian tomb are these words:

"His earthly tenement was shattered by beer and wine, and his spirit departed before it was called for."

One thousand years before Christ was made flesh and walked among men, Solomon gave this warning—a warning from human experience and from wisdom of God:

"Look not thou upon the wine when it is red, when it

giveth his color in the cup, when it moveth itself aright. At the last it biteth like a serpent and stingeth like an adder.''

In 550 B.C. Buddha gave a statement that flashed in that day as a zig-zag path of lightning:

''Drink not liquors that intoxicate and disturb the reason.''

And Xenophon, three-hundred years before heaven put out its brightest star to mark the birthplace of the incarnate Christ in Bethlehem, said:

''Temperance means first, moderation in healthful indulgence and, secondly, abstinence from things dangerous, as the use of intoxicating wines.''

And Pliny, the Elder, speaking words without the least semblance of foolishness, in 79 A.D., said:

''There is nothing about which we put ourselves to more trouble than wine, as if nature hath not given to us the most salubrious drink with which all other animals are satisfied.''

And Chaucer chastised the winebibber in 1340 with this statement:

''Character and shame depart when wine comes in.''

And Shakespeare, from whose pen words of wisdom dropped like golden pollen from the stems of shaken lilies, thrust the wine-drinking curse through with these words:

''O thou invisible spirit of wine, if thou hast no name to be known by, let us call thee devil!''

And Abraham Lincoln, in whose heart was no room for the memory of a wrong, in 1842, said:

''Liquor might have defenders, but no defense. Whether or not the world would be vastly benefited by a total and final banishment from it of all intoxicating drinks, seems to me not an open question.''

And Gladstone, who being dead yet speaketh in the parliaments of men, in 1898 said:

"The ravages of drink are greater than those of war, pestilence and famine combined."

And Cardinal Gibbons was not uttering a gibe when, in 1915, he spoke this sentence:

"This great curse of the labouring man is intemperance. It has brought more desolation to the wage earner than strikes or war or sickness or death. It has caused little children to be hungry and cold and to grow up among evil associations. It has broken up more homes and wrecked more lives than any other cause."

And George Clemenceau, put forth words of wisdom that cannot be weighed in scales when, in 1920, he declared:

"It is definitely settled that alcohol is a poison; a poison destructive of human energy and, for this reason, of society as a whole."

And Sir Wilfred Grenfell, whose name has been on the tongues of multitudes of English-speaking peoples, said:

"Alcohol has wrecked more lives, starved more children and murdered more women than any other single factor."

And Thomas Edison, scientist nonpareil, did not hesitate to declare:

"I still feel that prohibition is the greatest experiment yet made to benefit man."

And Chester Rowell, a man of no mean proportions, has well said:

"One drink is too many for the man at the automobile wheel, and the danger point is far short of the drunken point in nearly all of the occupations of life."

And Josephus Daniels, soldier in time of war, soldier in time of peace, said:

"The man who opposes prohibition and says in the next breath that he never could tolerate the return of the saloon, either is practicing deception or he does not know that as surely as night follows day, the fall of prohibition means the enthronement of the saloon.''

But, in the face of this verdict of the ages, and of Bible truth, and in the presence of multitudinous iniquities caused by strong drink, many clamor, with more noise than sense for personal liberty. Personal liberty! Liberty without love is a dangerous thing indeed. On all sides men must surrender liberties for the public welfare. There can be no peace in the home without consideration of others. There can be no profit in business without consideration of the welfare of others. There can be no justice in government and no safety in society without consideration for the welfare of others. There can be no happiness, no culture, no security anywhere without frank and sincere consideration of others—their comforts, their health, their prosperity, their rights.

Every city has fire limits. In certain districts only fire-proof construction can be used. Specifications for minutest details must be complied with before the foundation can be laid. Floors must be of concrete, roofs of slate. Why? Are not frame houses attractive? Certainly, but they could not be built in the crowded districts without endangering the entire community. They would be tinder boxes. Your liberty, your right to build a frame house which is thoroughly good of itself, and in its place, is removed *in the interest of public safety.*

You cannot *drive* where you will. You must obey the traffic laws. One poorly managed automobile often congests a crowded avenue for several minutes. One wild driver kills and maims.

You cannot *eat* what you will. The future builds upon the present. Today sanitoriums are crowded with dyspeptics who were the gormandisers of yesterday.

You cannot *walk* the streets of the city—if you have smallpox. Personal liberty ends.

Drink destroys the liberty of the drinker. See him

stagger and fall. He cannot direct his steps or rule his limbs. Hear him shout and curse. He does not know what he is saying, and has lost command of his thoughts and tongue. His eyes are dulled, his baser passions unleashed, his moral sense blunted, his better self chained. The drunkard, pitiable slave in body, mind and soul, is a refutation of the personal liberty plea.

Drink destroys the liberty of the drinker's wife and of his children. Is the bruised faced woman in ragged garments, lacking the necessities of life, free? Is the lad forced to wear the shame of the drunkard's child, free? Is the broken-hearted parent who mourns the death of a dissolute son in a saloon brawl or on the public highway or in the bootlegger's den, free? Is the child that receives in its body the ills of a drunkard's blood, free?

Shall we continue to respect the "personal liberty" of those who would destroy themselves and us? Shall we continue to respect the "personal liberty" of those who coin money from the tears of women and children and the cries of unfortunates possessed of a fiendish thirst they cannot master so long as the thing that arouses it survives because the law is violated?

They "are overcome with wine" (Isaiah 28:1). Men say they swallow strong drink. But strong drink swallows them—really. Strong drink eats up their substance. It eats their health. It swallows their happiness. It swallows many precious talents. A schoolboy in Australia some years ago put the matter tersely when he said, "I abstain from liquor because, if I wish to excel as a cricketer, Grace says, 'Abstain'; as a walker, Weston says, 'Abstain'; as an oarsman, Hanlon says, 'Abstain'; as a swimmer, Webb says, 'Abstain'; as a missionary, Livingstone says, 'Abstain'; as a doctor, Clark says, 'Abstain'; as a preacher, Farrar says, 'Abstain'!"

Strong drink does our schools and colleges no good.

It does our merchants no good. It does our manufacturers no good. It does our railroads no good. It does our churches no good. It does no man any good.

All I have written above is not strictly original. But what I have written is to give emphasis to all anybody says against strong drink and to make declaration that if I had one hair in my head that was in favor of strong drink "in any shape, form, or fashion" I would pull it out. And I take my stand with Guy Mark, who said,

"I am dry, bone-dry, because I have known unborn babes to be cursed through booze; little children to starve because of booze; young people to be stunted of life through booze; gifted women to become imbeciles through booze; leaders in industry to become beggars in the street because of booze; wedding rings to be sold for booze; every article of furniture to be pawned for booze; fortunes to be squandered for booze; girls to become prostitutes through booze; boys to become criminals through booze; women to be hanged because of booze; and men to go to the electric chair because of booze.

"Because I have never known booze to contribute to the happiness of a single child, or to the mental ability of a single young person, or to the moral uplift of a single middle-aged person, or to the comfort and blessedness of a single old person. Therefore, why shouldn't I be dry, bone-dry?"

Think of the disappointments that come in the path of wine. And remember what the Book hath said, namely,

Wine is a mocker, strong drink is raging; and whosoever is deceived thereby is not wise (Proverbs 20:1).

Hear thou, my son, and be wise, and guide thine heart in the way. Be not among winebibbers; among riotous eaters of flesh: for the drunkard and the glutton shall come to poverty: and drowsiness shall clothe a man with rags (Proverbs 23:19-21).

Woe unto him that giveth his neighbour drink, that puttest thy

bottle to him, and makest him drunk also, that thou mayest look
on their nakedness (Habbakuk 2:15).

Surely all this we have said will cause us to say from
our hearts that hooch is hellish, that booze is blasting,
that wine is wicked, that drink is damaging—now and
always.

It is not for kings, O Lemuel, it is not for kings to drink wine;
nor for princes strong drink. Lest they drink, and forget the law,
and pervert the judgment of any of the afflicted. Give strong drink
unto him that is ready to perish, and wine unto those that be of heavy
hearts (Proverbs 31:4-6).

Not having found the path of joy and peace which
his heart craved, Solomon traveled another path of disappointment. It was

III. THE PATH OF WEALTH

Moreover the profit of the earth is for all: the king himself is
served by the field. He that loveth silver shall not be satisfied with
silver; nor he that loveth abundance with increase; this is also vanity.
When goods increase, they are increased that eat them; and what
good is there to the owners thereof, saving the beholding of them
with their eyes? The sleep of the labouring man is sweet, whether
he eat little or much: but the abundance of the rich will not suffer
him to sleep. There is a sore evil which I have seen under the sun,
namely: riches kept for the owners thereof to their hurt. But those
riches perish by evil travail; and he begetteth a son, and there is
nothing in his hand (Ecclesiastes 5:9-15).

In these striking words we see that he also found the
path of riches a disappointing path. Finding bitterness
in the path of wine, finding no peace in human wisdom
alone, he turned to the path of riches, hoping therein to
find the joy and peace the human heart needs. Notice how
rich he was.

And they came to Ophir, and fetched from thence gold, four
hundred and twenty talents, and brought it to king Solomon (I Kings
9:28).

And the navy also of Hiram, that brought gold from Ophir, brought

in from Ophir great plenty of almug trees, and precious stones
(I Kings 10:11).

Now the weight of gold that came to Solomon in one year was
six hundred threescore and six talents of gold (I Kings 10:14).

And king Solomon made two hundred targets of beaten gold; six
hundred shekels of gold went to one target.

And he made three hundred shields of beaten gold; three pounds
of gold went to one shield; and the king put them in the house of
the forest of Lebanon (I Kings 10:16, 17).

Besides that he had of the merchantmen and of the traffic of spice
merchants, and of all the kings of Arabia, and of the governors of
the country (I Kings 10:15).

For the king had at sea a navy of Tarshish with the navy of
Hiram: once every three years came the navy of Tarshish, bringing
gold, and silver, ivory, and apes, and peacocks (I Kings 10:22).

And the king made silver to be Jerusalem as stones, and cedars
made he to be the sycomore trees that are in the vale, for abundance
(I Kings 10:27).

He had a great house which took over thirteen years
to build.

But Solomon was building his own house thirteen years, and he
finished all his house (I Kings 7:1).

He had a great house in the forest of Lebanon also.

He built also the house of the forest of Lebanon; the length
thereof was an hundred cubits, and the breadth thereof fifty cubits,
and the height thereof thirty cubits, upon four rows of cedar pillars,
with cedar beams upon the pillars (I Kings 7:2).

He had many singers and musicians.

And the king made of the almug trees pillars for the house of
the Lord, and for the king's house, harps also and psalteries for
singers: there came no such almug trees, nor were seen unto this
day (I Kings 10:12).

He had a great throne of ivory.

Moreover the king made a great throne of ivory, and overlaid it
with the best gold. The throne had six steps, and the top of the throne
was round behind: and there were stays on either side on the place
of the seat, and two lions stood beside the stays. And twelve lions

stood there on the one side and on the other upon the six steps: there was not the like made in any kingdom (I Kings 10:18-20).

He had many drinking vessels.

And all king Solomon's drinking vessels were of gold, and all the vessels of the house of the forest of Lebanon were of pure gold; none were of silver: it was nothing accounted of in the days of Solomon (I Kings 10.21).

He had many who brought him rich gifts.

And Solomon reigned over all kingdoms from the river unto the land of the Philistines, and unto the bordor of Egypt; they brought presents, and served Solomon all the days of his life (I Kings 4:21).

And they brought every man his present, vessels of silver, and vessels of gold, and garments, and armour, and spices, horses, and mules, a rate year by year (I Kings 10:25).

He had forty thousand horses in his livery stables, and fourteen hundred chariots, and twelve thousand horsemen.

And Solomon had forty thousand stalls of horses for his chariots, and twelve thousand horsemen (I Kings 4:26).

And Solomon gathered together chariots and horsemen; and he had a thousand and four hundred chariots, and twelve thousand horsemen, whom he bestowed in the cities for chariots, and with the king at Jerusalem (I Kings 10:26).

He had just one day's provision in the kitchen the following:

And Solomon's provision for one day was thirty measures of fine flour, and threescore measures of meal. Ten fat oxen, and twenty oxen out of the pastures, and an hundred sheep, beside harts, and roebucks, and fallowdeer, and fatted fowl (I Kings 4:22, 23).

So king Solomon exceeded all the kings of the earth for riches and for wisdom (I Kings 10:23).

Yes, gifts poured into his coffers in a continuous stream, so that he was able to hire men singers and women singers—able to build himself and his wives gorgeous palaces—able to enjoy all that money could provide. He was able at any time to pay a king's ransom for a day of pleasure. He had riches till the end of his life. He never knew the pinch of poverty—never knew any anxiety about his daily bread. Yet, even in the security of his nest of wealth, he fully realized the futility of their values. "Vanity of vanities!"

No man can *buy* a contented heart. Money is powerless to furnish this. No man can purchase with riches a soul at peace with God. No man can pay in money the price of the hope of immortality and of a meeting in the great beyond. No man can find in riches the purchase price of God's favor or the realization of eternal salvation. Not even in this day does money guarantee health, or hold friends, or bring contentment!

They that will be rich fall into a temptation and a snare, and into many foolish and hurtful lusts, which drown men in destruction and perdition (I Timothy 6:9).

Go to, now, ye rich men, weep and howl for your miseries that shall come upon you. Your riches are corrupted, and your garments are motheaten. Your gold and silver is cankered, and the rust of them shall be a witness against you, and shall eat your flesh as it were fire (James 5:1-3).

Labour not to be rich: cease from thine own wisdom? Wilt thou set thine eyes upon that which is not? for riches certainly make themselves wings; they fly away as an eagle toward heaven (Proverbs 23:4, 5).

Disappointed in these three paths, Solomon turned to

IV. The Path of Works

Wisdom, the many things he knew, brought him not to the house of abiding happiness—brought him not that joy which is ever rich and abiding. Wine turned out to be a mocker, as it always does—mocking him with the shadow instead of the substance of good things, mocking him with the desert where it promised an oasis. And wealth had no power to satisfy. Amid all his abundance there was a lack—something that rested not and was not still, something that hungered and was not fed, something that was thirsty and found no satisfaction.

Solomon built palaces. Solomon established great public works. Solomon increased the size and magnificence of his city. Solomon transported forests. He did mighty things in the matter of building cities and other great public works. He accomplished such things as multitudes have expected to provide satisfaction for life's labors. But when he had finished all his great works he looked out upon them and cried, "Vanity of vanities!"

For he had dominion over all the region on this side the river Tiphsah even to Azzah, over all the kings on this side the river: and he had peace on all sides round about him (I Kings 4:24).

And Solomon's wisdom excelled the wisdom of all the children of the east country, and all the wisdom of Egypt. For he was wiser than all men; than Ethan the Ezrahite, and Heman, and Chalcol, and Darde, the sons of Mahol; and his fame was in all nations round about (I Kings 4:30, 31).

But Solomon was building his own house thirteen years, and he finished all his house. He built also the house of the forest of Lebanon; the length thereof was an hundred cubits, and the breadth thereof fifty cubits, and the height thereof thirty cubits, upon four rows of cedar pillars, with cedar beams upon the pillars. And it was covered with cedar above upon the beams, they lay on forty-five pillars, fifteen in a row. And there were windows in three rows, and light against light in three ranks. And all the doors and posts were square, with the windows: and light was against light in three ranks. And he made a porch of pillars; the length thereof was fifty cubits, and the breadth thereof thirty cubits: and the porch was before them; and the other pillars and the thick beam were before them. Then he made a porch for the throne where he might judge, even the porch of judgment: and it was covered with cedar from one side the floor to the other. And his house where he dwelt had another court within the porch, which was of the like work. Solomon made also an house for Pharaoh's daughter, whom he had taken to wife, like unto his porch. And these were of costly stones, according to the measures of hewed stones, sawed with saws, within and without, even from the fountain unto the coping, and so on the outside toward the great court. And the foundation was of costly stones, even great stones, stones of ten cubits, and stones of eight cubits. And above were costly stones, after the measure of hewed stones and cedars. And the great court round about was with three rows of hewed stones and a row of cedar beams, both for the inner court of the house of the Lord and for the porch of the house (I Kings 7:1-12).

And Solomon built Gezer, and Beth-horon the nether, and Baalath, and Tadmor in the wilderness, in the land, and all the cities of store that Solomon had, and cities for his chariots, and cities for his horsemen, and that which Solomon desired to build in Jerusalem, and in Lebanon, and in all the land of his dominion (I Kings 9:17-19).

When the queen of Sheba saw all the wonders of the works Solomon had brought to pass, it startled her. The Bible, in I Kings 10:1-8, tells us how she was completely dumfounded when she saw it all. Hear it:

And when the queen of Sheba heard of the fame of Solomon concerning the name of the Lord, she came to prove him with hard questions. And she came to Jerusalem with a very great train, with camels that bare spices, and very much gold, and precious stones: and when she was come to Solomon, she communed with him of all that was in her heart.

And Solomon told her all her questions: there was not anything hid from the king, which he told her not. And when the queen of Sheba had seen all Solomon's wisdom, and the house he had built, and the meat of his table, and the sitting of his servants, and the attendance of his ministers, and their apparel, and his cupbearers, and his ascent by which he went up into the house of the Lord; there was no more spirit in her. And she said to the king, It was a true report I heard in mine own land of thy acts and of thy wisdom. Howbeit I believed not the words, until I came, and mine eyes had seen it: and, behold, the half was not told me: thy wisdom and prosperity exceedeth the fame which I heard. Happy are thy men, happy are thy servants, which stand continually before thee, and that hear thy wisdom (I Kings 10:1-8).

All of which brings us to pray:

So teach us to number our days, that we may apply our hearts unto wisdom.

O satisfy us early with thy mercy; that we may rejoice and be glad all our days.

Let thy work appear unto thy servants, and thy story unto their children. And let the beauty of the Lord our God be upon us: and establish thou the work of our hands upon us; yea, the work of our hands establish thou it (Psalms 90:12, 14, 16, 17).

Which, moreover, brings us the willingness to obey the exhortation given in I Cor. 15:58, namely,

Therefore, my beloved brethren, be ye steadfast, unmovable, always abounding in the work of the Lord, forasmuch as ye know that your labour is not in vain in the Lord.

But Solomon trod another disappointment. It was

V. The Path of Women

When Solomon found disappointment in the path of wisdom, in the path of wine, in the path of wealth, in the path of great works of construction, he turned to seek happiness with women. With much wisdom given him, he played the fool with women. With much opportunity to do good, he delighted himself in indulgence with women. With the power to command and to persuade, with the whole world from which to choose, with wealth that was enticing, he strove to delight his heart with women.

But king Solomon loved many strange women, together with the daughter of Pharaoh, women of the Moabites, Ammonites, Edomites, Zidonians, and Hittites; of the nations concerning which the Lord said unto the children of Israel, Ye shall not go in to them, neither shall they come in unto you: for surely they will turn away your heart after their gods: Solomon clave unto these in love. And he had seven hundred wives, princesses, and three hundred concubines: and his wives turned away his heart. For it came to pass, when Solomon was old, that his wives turned away his heart after other gods; and his heart was not perfect with the Lord his God, as was the heart of David his father. For Solomon went after Ashtoreth the goddess of the Zidonians, and after Milcom the abomination of the Ammonites. And Solomon did evil in the sight of the Lord, and went not fully after the Lord, as did David his father. Then did Solomon build an high place for Chemosh, the abomination of Moab, in the hill that is before Jerusalem, and for Molech, the abomination of the children of Ammon. And likewise did he for all his strange wives, which burnt incense and sacrificed unto their gods (I Kings 11:1-8).

Solomon knew what he was talking about when he said,

Give not thy strength unto women (Proverbs 31:3).

Solomon was speaking from the depths of bitter experience, teaching that the reproofs of instruction are the way of life, when he said:

My son, keep thy father's commandment, for forsake not the law of thy mother. Bind them continually upon thine heart, and tie them about thy neck.

When thou goest, it shall lead thee; when thou sleepest, it shall keep thee; and when thou awakest, it shall talk with thee. For the commandment is a lamp; and the law is light; and the reproofs of instruction are the way of life; to keep thee from the evil women, from the flattery of the tongue of a strange woman. Lust not after her beauty in thine heart; neither let her take thee with her eyelids. For by means of a whorish woman a man is brought to a piece of bread; and the adulteress will hunt for the precious life. Can a man take fire in his bosom, and his clothes not be burned? Can one go upon hot coals, and his feet not be burned? (Proverbs 6:20-28).

But whoso committeth adultery with a woman lacketh understanding; he that doeth it destroyeth his own soul.

A wound and dishonour shall he get; and his reproach shall not be wiped away (Proverbs 6:32, 33).

Solomon had found out that in the path of women there is that experience that is as vinegar to the teeth and as smoke to the eyes. That is why he wrote:

A foolish woman is clamorous; she is simple and knoweth nothing. For she sitteth at the door of her house, on a seat in the high places of the city, to call passengers who go right on their ways: whoso is simple, let him turn in hither: and as for him that wanteth understanding, she saith to him, stolen waters are sweet, and bread eaten in secret is pleasant. But he knoweth not that the dead are there; and that her guests are in the depths of hell (Proverbs 9:13-18).

It was Solomon, Solomon who had seven hundred wives, who said:

A virtuous woman is a crown to her husband: but she that maketh ashamed is as rottenness in his bones (Proverbs 12:4).

It is better to dwell in the corner of the house top, than with a brawling woman on a wide house (Proverbs 21:9).

It is better to dwell in the wilderness, than with a contentious and an angry woman (Proverbs 21:19).

It was Solomon, the king with riches, who, after much indulgence with women, said:

For a whore is a deep ditch; and a strange woman is a narrow pit. She also lieth in wait as for prey, and increaseth the transgressors among men (Proverbs 23:27, 28).

It was Solomon who said many lovely things about women, lovely things which were true altogether, such as:

Whoso findeth a wife findeth a good thing and obtaineth favour of the Lord (Proverbs 18:22).

A prudent wife is from the Lord (Proverbs 19:14).

Who can find a virtuous woman? for her price is far above rubies (Proverbs 31:10).

She will do him good and not evil all the days of her life (Proverbs 31:12).

A woman that feareth the Lord, she shall be praised (Proverbs 31:30).

A virtuous woman is a crown to her husband (Proverbs 12:4).

But he also said:

It is better to dwell in the corner of the house top, than with a brawling woman in a wide house (Proverbs 21:9).

It is better to dwell in the wilderness, than with a contentious and an angry woman (Proverbs 21:19).

And this truth, he uttered in language descriptive of ancient day indulgence and descriptive also of this jazz-day indulgence:

Say unto wisdom, Thou art my sister; and call understanding thy kinswoman; that they may keep thee from the strange woman, from the stranger which flattereth with her words. For at the window of my house I looked through my casement, and beheld among the simple ones, I discerned among the youths, a young man void of understanding, passing through the street near her corner; and he went the way to her house, in the twilight, in the evening, in the black and dark night, and behold there met him a woman with the attire of an harlot, and subtil of heart. (She is loud and stubborn; her feet abide not in her house: now is she without, now in the streets, and lieth in wait at every corner). So she caught him, and kissed him, and with an impudent face said unto him, I have peace offerings with me; this day have I payed my vows. Therefore came I forth to meet thee, diligently to seek thy face, and I have found thee. I have decked my bed with coverings of tapestry, with carved works, with fine linen of Egypt. I have perfumed my bed with myrrh, aloes and cinnamon. Come, let us take our fill of love until the morning: let us solace ourselves with loves. For the good man is not at home, he is gone a long journey: He hath taken a bag of money with him, and will come at the day appointed. With her much fair speech she caused him to yield, with the flattering of her lips she forced him. He goeth after her straightway, as an ox goeth to the slaughter, or as a fool to the correction of the stocks; till a dart strike through his liver; as a bird hasteth to the snare, and knoweth not that it is for his life. Hearken unto me now therefore, O ye children, and attend to the words of my mouth. Let not thine heart decline to her ways, go not astray in her paths. For she hath cast down many wounded: yea, many strong men have been slain by her. Her house is the way to hell, going down to the chambers of death (Proverbs 7:4-27).

To all of which I, with prayer and purpose to do good, especially to any young man who may read and who may have fallen into indulgence with the evil woman, would add:

> A woman is waiting for you, my lad—
>   Ride past!
> Her cheeks are soft and her mouth is glad—
>   Ride past!
> For the flash of her glance is the light of bane,
> And the touch of her lips is the key to pain,
> And she calls to the wise men—all in vain!
> But youth is strong and will find no wrong
> In the lilting lure of her ancient song.

And the thing that's **art**, and the thing that's **heart**,
Only the knowing can tell apart;
And the price of the knowledge is black with stain,
And the seed of the wisdom, bad.

She would barter her love for your own, my lad—
　Ride past!
But your love is good and her love is bad—
　Ride past!
She offers the fruit of the bitter tree,
Her kiss is the promise of misery,
Of death and of woe; let her be! let her be!
Youth is bold and of eager mold,
And brass in the ken of youth is **gold**,
And the acid of grief is the only test
For the tawdry tinsel within her breast—
Which only the eyes of the wise can see—
And the eyes of the wise are sad!

What has not woman meant to man? She is the synonym of all that is holy in religion—synonym of all that is encouraging, stimulating, and soothing in life's stress and sorrows. Woman—God's loveliest gift to man. God pity the man who, in the dark hour of his dissolution, has no woman's hand to wipe away the death damp from his brow, or to smooth his pillow, and no woman's voice to whisper sweet words of cheer and comfort into his fast dulling ear. So said one. So say we all.

Woman—synonym of home and love, of wifehood, of motherhood, of sisterhood, of daughterhood.

Woman—synonym of all gentleness, of charm, of winsomeness, of heart's ease, of sacrificial service.

Woman—the uncomplaining bearer of burdens, the partner of pain and pleasure alike, the keeper of the mysteries of life, the fount of joy, the confidante of weakness and of sorrow, the sharer of tears and laughter.

Woman—she means to the race all that men's hearts have yearned for, in rest from labor, in refuge from defeat, in comfort from sorrow, in understanding and encouragement, in reproach, in cheer and encouragement in struggle.

Many times Solomon doubtless proved all this, for he was a married man. And yet, because he left God out and reckoned not with His laws in relation to women, he found the path of women a path of great disappointments. "Having tried all the avenues of legitimate love; he tried the other way. And so great was the disappointment and bitterness, he was constrained to cry, 'Vanity of vanities!' Having tried all the delights of legitimate love, he then indulged himself in all the fancied pleasure of illegitimate love, and excitation of unholy desire and indulgence of animal appetite—the pursuance of purely fleshly pleasure. Here, too, for his joy he reaped ashes. Here, too, he found his honey turned to the bitterness of gall. Here, too, in these wide avenues of all illegitimate dealings with women, his delight faded into distaste and disgust! Here, too, desire became despair. And again his soul was wrung with the cry that has saddened the centuries—'Vanity of vanities!' "

Which brings us to speak of

VI. OUR ONE HOPE

The world by wisdom knew not God (I Cor. 1:21).

Poor rich Solomon. Poor fool-wise-man Solomon. Poor wine-tasting Solomon. Type of all our wisdom—in the slough of despond. Type of all our indulgence—in dark, abysmal despair. Type of all man's wrong indulgence with women—surfeited with disgust. For man's effort to find peace and happiness by the paths of wisdom and wine and wealth and works and women is written in the lives of men. The coarseness, the sensuousness, the unspirituality seen about us is tragic.

But God is ever the God of the second chance. It is ever the providence of his mercy, if we will turn from our wicked ways, to reverse the curse of sin. Then—do this. Through Jesus who died for you—do this. With faith in the Christ who bore our sins in His own body on the tree (I Peter 2:24), and died the just for the unjust that He might bring us to God (I Peter 3:18)—embrace the cross now. Then the cry of your despair will be turned into joy. Then the consciousness of your lost estate will be changed into the sweet and blessed realization of eternal salvation. Whatever unsightliness of sin, whatever hardness and impenitence of heart, whatever uncouthness of spiritual experience in your life intervenes between what you are and what you would be, bring the Master to view it. See it through His eyes. Get His viewpoint. He will make you a new creature. And the work He thus begins He will continue to its full completion, so that not only you, but He Himself will be satisfied with His working in your soul.

There shall be no disappointment with you concerning Him. There will be no disappointment with Him concerning you.

CHAPTER 3

CHRIST, MY ONLY NECESSITY

Jesus only (Matthew 17:8).

I am not come to praise Jesus. A sense of woeful inadequacy, falling oppressively upon the heart, forbids that. For architects, straining their powers to the utmost, conceive no cathedrals great enough for His worship. Painters, holding cargoes of wonder in their brushes, paint no pictures beautiful enough to depict Him. Sculptors, searching through all quarries, find no marble white enough for His brow. Musicians, making surging seas of tone subservient to their batons, create no compositions sweet enough for His hymns of praise. Orators, whose words are flights of golden arrows, reach only the outskirts of His grandeur. Poets, sweeping their thoughts together in poems and dramas, measure Him but feebly. Writers, wielding pens that are fountain heads of a Niagara, express only meagre measure of the honor due Him.

> Oh, who shall paint him? Let the sweetest tone,
> That ever trembled on the harps of heaven
> Be discord; let the chanting seraphim
> Whose anthem is eternity be dumb;
> For praise and wonder, adoration, all
> Melt into muteness ere they soar to thee
> The sole perfection! Theme of countless worlds!

But, by the law of first things, by the claims of time and eternity, by your desire to consider the loftiest concerns of the soul, by the acknowledged tendency of many to turn back because some new menace has robbed them of their courage, by the necessity to bring each task and duty a life of uttermost consecration, by the proneness of many youths to live under a perilously low pressure, by the lure to drop the old moralities in the novel demands of a new world—by all these things, I am bound to the privileged task of speaking on how Christ, who attaches a value to the soul beyond that of the whole world, who shoots life through and through with sacredness, is available and sufficient for every material, mental, and moral necessity of life, satisfying every need of our being.

I speak to youth tonight. You have youth—the best, the most dangerous gift of life. Young, you have the privilege of placing finger-marks upon mighty history-making events. Your capital has not been wasted in unprofitable investments. Wealth that you can put out at a high rate of interest and an infinite capacity for the joy that is ever rich and abiding is yours. You have not experienced the weight of years and the departure of unrecoverable strength! Therefore, what glories await you in this wonderful age!

I speak to students tonight. Your minds travel to the uttermost parts in time and space. You hear the eloquence of world-famed orators, ponder the wisdom of the greatest philosophers, recount the glory of ancient nations, march with Caesar's armies, join Napoleon's campaigns, sit in the world's greatest councils. You are to see light and liberty supersede superstitions and negations, to hear the tread of men moving to freedom! You are to learn Nature's secrets and share the power that makes her forces messengers and untiring slaves of humanity. To Dante, Shakespeare, Virgil, Homer, you talk across great distances. With Raphael, Rembrandt, Titian, Millet, you paint. Beethoven, Mozart, Mendelssohn, you hear as they build rhythmic palaces of melody before the eyes of the soul.

But how little this will avail if, in accumulating knowledge, you learn not that Jesus is the way, the truth, the life, and that, having Him, you need nothing more. For you have in Him all that is essential to Christianity. How little value will come to you of the treasures of knowledge if you are not "filled with the knowledge of His will in all wisdom and spiritual understanding, that you might walk worthy of the Lord unto all pleasing, being fruitful in every good work, and increasing in the knowledge of God, strengthened with all might according to His glorious power."

What profit if, in study, we find not God in His most glorious manifestations? If, at the end of the microscope's journey, we see not His infinitesimal care? If, in the findings of the telescope, we see not His infinite greatness? If, in mathematics and the sciences, we learn not of His immutable ways? If, in the fields of botany and in the kingdom of music, we glimpse not His ineffable beauty? If, scrutinizing the rocks of geology, we learn not the testimony of His incomprehensible agelessness? If, in amassing knowledge, we miss the spiritual meaning of a college education and have no enriching experience of Jesus?

For how measly a price you will sell a glorious future if you do not have a rich equipment of responsiveness to the truth that only in Christ you will find the true and rich way in life and reach the possession of power.

Power!

That word expresses the most insistent cry of our age. Who is ashamed of power? Nobody. In *that* all people exult. Engines of power, motors of power, explosives of power, athletes of power, armies of power, intellects

of power! In these we take great pride. And we have
covert admiration for Ghandi because, with all his
faults he is a man of power. Men cry out for power
—power to realize the natural kingdom—to conquer it, reign over it, utilize it, enjoy it. But moral
and spiritual power is the world's need today. We have
no adequate power house when we draw our power from
ideals, from philosophies, rather than from a living
Personality who is Himself "the fountain life," who will
pour the floods of His own vitality into our impoverished
souls. Which is to say, there is only one secret of personal
power. The secret is in Jesus Christ. With all its wealth,
its scientific power, its modern ideas, the world today
has no substitute for Jesus Christ. He meets all needs
of these tremendous days. He is adequate for life in
every situation.

More than material energy, we need the power to
realize ourselves gloriously, to make possible the marvelous things of the highest life—in the material, mental,
and spiritual realm. For a power effectual to the attain-
ment of the highest life all serious souls yearn. Power not
from the earth, but from the earth's Creator.

Not from the sea, but from Him who walked upon its
tumbling waters.

Not from the winds, but from Him who rides upon its
wings.

Not from the sun, but from Him who lit its fires.

Not from the clouds, but from Him who maketh the
clouds His chariots.

Not from the stars, but from Him who allied them
against Sisera.

The power of the Highest to transcend our painful
limitations, to renew our deranged and deteriorated
capacities, to make us equal to the sublime of character
and duty. That power.

Great is the claim the New Testament makes that in Christ Jesus this power is made ours.

So! Christ is our only necessity for the fulness of supply and power in

I. The Physical Realm

A large place is given the body in the New Testament. While the Bible insists upon the soul with much urgency, it casts glory upon the body. "Know ye not that your body is a temple of the Holy Ghost . . . ?" (I Cor. 6:19). "I beseech you . . . that ye present your bodies a living sacrifice, holy, acceptable unto God" (Rom. 12:1). "Glorify God in your body" (I Cor. 6:20). "He is the saviour of the body" (Eph. 5:23).

Such statements, inwrought in the web of Scripture, teach us that the Word of God in Christ is the true charter of the human body. By the coming of God in human form, Jesus, clothed the body with imperishable nobility. By Him who was made flesh, whose every muscle was a pulley divinely swung, whose every nerve was divine handwriting, whose every bone was divine sculpture, who, in kingly fashion, wore the flesh as a garment, the body has been made an instrument of Christ. Through the human mouth God in authority spoke. Through human eyes God in pity looked. Through human hands God in love wrought. Upon human feet God on errands of mercy went. Through a human heart God's compassion was shown. Through human ears God heard humanity's despairing cry.

The body, our constant companion, is the basis of all men's manifold activities. Many victims of the errors of monasticism have ignored the body, giving attention only to the soul. Many looking upon the body as essentially evil have set all the militant energies of their personality in battle array against its assertion of supremacy. Many allowing the spirit to abdicate and the body to sit on the throne have surrendered to the body. But through Christ, not through the rigid austerity of the ascetic, the uplift of the body come. Not through the indulgence of the voluptuary, but through Christ we find manifold satisfactions and satisfactory life for the body—get rid of the wrong attitude that labels the body a foe rather than the friend of the spiritual life—pass from the feverishness of *living* to the more blessed experience of *life*.

> Seated within this body's car,
>   The silent self is driven far,
>   And the five senses at the pole,
> Like steeds are tugging restive of control.
>
> And if the driver lose his way
>   Or the reins break, who can say
>   Into what blind paths, what pits of fear
> Will plunge the chargers in their mad career?

Only in Christ is such a mad career of the body, as Carlyle here depicts, prevented, and all members of the body are made servants of a loving will, representatives of kindly thought, ambassadors of a great heart, and instruments of righteousness in His service.

> God gave him passions splendid as the sun
> Meant for the lordliest purposes—a part
> Of Nature's full and fertile mother's heart,
> From which new systems and new worlds are spun.
> And now behold! Behold what he has done!
> In Folly's court and Carnal Pleasure's mart
> He flung the wealth God gave him at the start.
> At dawn he stood potential, opulent,
> With virile manhood and emotions keen.
> At noon he stands—all Love's fortune spent
> In petty traffic, unproductive, mean—
> A pauper cursed with impotent desire!

Only in Christ is such waste as Mrs. Wilcox here indicates prevented—the body made the vehicle of moral and spiritual meanings, the instrument of the Unseen and the Eternal, the channel through which the Divine becomes articulate. And thus the physical reaches the climax of its development. It becomes the visible expression of invisible values, is dominated by commanding and noble sanctions, and is made a friend to be welcomed to the activities of the great moral and spiritual tasks of life. Made an instrument through which the invisible splendors of the spiritual world becomes visible. Thus the body abides in fruitfulness. All its energies, wholesome and noble in themselves, become the vehicle of the great eternal realities.

Hough was right who said, "The gospel of the physical life as an ally of the spiritual vitalities will change the world for multitudes of young people who, flooded with knowledge of physical processes, have come to think of the body as the foe of the invisible splendors of the life of the spirit."

Christ, our only necessity, who guides the physical to its true and normal life in the service of the spiritual, said to His disciples, "I am with you alway." Thus He speaks to us today. And as those first faithfuls were charged with responsibilities for the message of Christ's kingdom in their day, so we are called to be Christians and charged with giving his message by word and life in this fateful hour.

His physical feet no longer press the highways and bypaths of earth. *We* must be His feet. His physical eyes no longer look upon Jerusalem. *We* must be His eyes. His physical voice no longer cries "Come unto me." *We* must be His voice. Christ's physical hands no longer minister. *We* must be His hands. If Christ has a physical presence today, He has it through us!

Hillis was right who said that persons, not abstractions, exalt. Not his reflections upon truth and beauty, but Socrates himself embodying these, transformed Athenian disciples. Not his theses on the church door at Wittenberg, but Luther's flaming heart changed Germany. Not Puritanism as a theory, but Puritanism incarnated in Cromwell and Hampden transformed England. Not a written declaration, but that declaration organized into Washington, Adams, and Jefferson and others less known but no less worthy wrought out our independence.

The God who once walked with holy men of old still works through Christians who, as soldiers of the Cross, would conquer the world for Christ, through Christian physicians who would keep the world in wisdom, through Christian statesmen who would keep the world in law, through Christian manufacturers who make God a partner in business, through Christian poets and prophets who would inspire and lead the people.

It is only when the Christ of this method lives in you, and you in Him, that you will find the sure way, know the real truth, reach the fullness of your possibilities, possess power. You need to seek no other way, no other truth to hold, no other life to desire than that which in Christ is realized.

No man really lives without this conception of life. Some are trying to do it. But they are dead—as dead as Lazarus. Yes, deader, for they have been dead for years where Lazarus was dead only four days.

Christ is the way; without him men are Cains, wanderers, vagabonds.

Christ is the truth; without him men are liars like the devil of old.

Christ is the life; without him men are dead.

Christ is the light; without him men are in darkness and go they know not whither.

Christ is the vine; without him men are withered branches.

Christ is the rock; without him men are carried away with the flood!

Out in Memphis we sat to catch the broadcast as the King of England opened the conference on disarmament.

Something in connection with it thrills my still soul. A small room in New York City was carefully prepared to receive the short wave and broadcast it to America. The apparatus was all set up and ready! A moment before the king's speech was to commence, a careless workman passing through the room tripped on the connecting wire and broke it. Mr. Vivian, in charge of the apparatus, saw the situation. He knew that it would take twenty minutes to go to the workrooms and get material to mend the wire. The king's speech would be gone. Vivian sprang forward, gripped one end of the wire in one hand and held the other end in his other hand for twenty minutes and let the message go through his body. For twenty minutes Vivian was the connecting link to receive that message of the king, broadcast in this country, a message of peace.

The King of kings and Lord of Lords has a message of infinite peace for the world, but it must pass, to be most effective, through our bodies!

"Let not sin therefore reign in your mortal body, that ye should obey it in the lusts thereof. Neither yield ye your members as instruments of unrighteousness unto sin: but yield yourselves unto God, as those that are alive from the dead, and your members as instruments of righteousness unto God" (Rom. 6:12, 13).

Since this is the need He has for us, He will supply all the material necessities of life. When your life is wholly surrendered to Him, not one key withheld, not one acre in the fields withheld for selfish use, not one room in the house locked against his entrance, He will supply all your need. Whatever that need is, no matter how deep and heartfelt that need may be, He will out of His infinite resources supply the material necessities. For this very thing Christ is our only necessity. That was when He supplied wine at Cana's wedding, when He fed thousands with a lad's lunch, when He put tax money in

the fish's mouth for Peter, when He filled the empty net.
The man or woman who trusts God will be tested—tried.
But God, who kept the cruse of oil from failing and the
handful of meal from wasting, commanded the ravens
to feed Elijah, gave manna to multitudes in the desert,
and made as brass the shoes of His people, will, through
Christ, never forsake or forget you.

Not only so. Jesus is our only necessity for reaching
the fulness of our possibilities in realms of

II. THE MENTAL

Jesus, who exalted character above reputation, religion
above ritual, substance above form, reality above appear-
ance, opens the door of high thought and mental achievement to us. From the intellectual conceit unaware of the
rattle of its dry bones, from the superficial mental illum-
ination that lacks the urge of sacrificial passion, from
the tragedy of contracting spiritual boundries while
extending intellectual frontiers, He delivers. He makes it
so that no matter what man and circumstance do to you
outwardly, they cannot prevent you from living inwardly
in the companionship of high thoughts. He opens the
doors which nobody can shut. The Roman Empire could
put narrow limitations around John's body, but it could
put no narrow limitations around John's mind. Marooned
on Patmos, he saw a new heaven and a new earth wherein dwelleth righteousness. Through Christ Paul, in
prison, could say, "Whatsoever things are true ... honest
... just ... pure ... lovely ... of good report ... *think* on
these things!" In prison, John Bunyan's mind roved
earth and heaven. And he wrote a book that escaped that
jail, traveled more highways and walked more bypaths
and knocked at more doors and spoke to more people
in their mother tongue than any book save the Bible.

In the mental realm Christ, Son of man without sin, Son of God with power, sets before thee an open door to high and effective thought, and no man can shut it— a door to straight thinking. You cannot afford to think crookedly. A farmer cannot. If he does, he will reap no harvests. Nor can the builder. If he does, his structure will collapse. Nor the artist, or his picture will be out of proportion and perspective and without proper coloring. The doctor cannot. He must think and think correctly before he gives medicine or takes the knife, or he is criminally guilty!

Many young people, adventurers in the kingdom of thought, today are asking if Jesus belongs only to the past, if He is an ideal figure "melting into a golden haze," if He is a retreating figure sailing away from us on the wooden vessel of the Cross over a bitter ocean into the unknown. They are asking if Christ has present power, if He has a word for us here and now, in our current problems.

Yes, He is here. Yes, He has present power. He is more than the Christ of history—a blessed memory. He is more than the Christ of prophecy—a sublime hope. He is the Christ of today, and of every day—a living reality in our lives. And to Him there is no Doubting Castle, no Slough of Despond, no Valley of Despair, no Hill of Difficulty. His rule is not the working of an experience of complicated numbers. Nor is His throne ice, His heart marble, His arm iron. His laws are no man-traps. He is not a cold, vague, far-off one, caring only that the wheels turn and the mills grind.

If you have a perplexity *now*, take it to Jesus; He will solve it. If you are held by a fear *now*, take it to Jesus; He will conquer it. If you are confused by the noise and tumult around you *now*, go to Jesus and you will find peace. If you are weighed down by the thoughts of your past sins, take them to Jesus, and the burden will be taken off. If you are lonely *now*, go to Jesus and you will find in Him the most glorious comradeship. If you are poor, He will pour the true wealth into your lap. All wisdom, all power, all peace, all joy are yours for the asking, only go to Jesus.

So! By Him in whom are hid all the treasures of wisdom, your minds will have the climate of perpetual ice that preserves them from the decay of *rotten* thoughts. And the climate of fire that prevents the cold of *loveless* thoughts. And the antidote that saves from the poison of *evil* thoughts. And the liberty that frees from the tyranny of *wrong* thoughts. And the perfume that sweetens from *foul* thoughts. All this shall be the climate of the mind—the frigid, the torrid, the temperate zones all bearing abundant fruit under Him.

The charge is made that the character of Jesus was effeminate—that He followed the line of least resistance. But strength of character is seen in a life that can dominate great minds.

Gladstone was great! But in Christ Gladstone's mighty intellect found anchorage, his impetuous temper restraint, his versatile personality fulfillment.

The strength of Woodrow Wilson can be seen in the great minds that He dominated. But Jesus dominated Wilson.

Martin Luther went to the Diet of Worms declaring he would go there "though there were as many devils as there were tiles on the housetops!" And there he stated his position. Was Luther courageous? Yes, but Jesus Christ dominated Luther.

John Calvin told the libertines of Geneva to shoot him in his pulpit if they dared, but that he would gladly fall on that open Bible in that pulpit for his Lord's sake. Courageous Calvin! But Jesus dominated Calvin.

Great the courage of John Knox whose preaching made

the queen declare that she feared him more than all the armies of Scotland! But Jesus dominated Knox.

Spurgeon, intellectual giant, soared like an eagle, sang like a lark preaching God's gospel. But Jesus dominated Spurgeon's great mind.

Carroll, reaching from pole to pole with his mighty mental wings, was dominated by Jesus.

What of John the Baptist? He was a hero who dared valiantly, a seer who saw clearly, a great heart who felt deeply! Jesus pronounced him the greatest born of woman. But John said he had need to be baptized of Jesus!

What of Paul? Thrilling life of hardship, hazard, heroism! Stoned for preaching, he preached on. He compassed the earth with the truths of redemption. He left a trail of glory across the Gentile world. Who dominated Paul? He answers that question in these words, "I count all things but loss . . . that I may know him and the power of his resurrection and the fellowship of his suffering."

We are a highly gifted, achieving, wealthy race. But much of what we call clothes has left us naked; much of what we call food has left us hungry; much of what is called satisfaction has never touched the sources of desire. But emotional awakenings calling for peace, spiritual outreach needing power, intellectual aspirations for truth—all, all are satisfied in Jesus. Every faculty of man finds food for joy—in Christ!

No man is fitted for living by a course in the arts and sciences. A man may know all the literature, speak all the languages, understand all the methods of the laboratories, be familiar with all the political economies, and in the end be nothing more than a modern Mephistopheles. Much learning is as unsatisfactory as fruits of Hesperides unless there be character free from the malefic spell of religious indifference and supercilious intellectuality.

In amassing knowledge, some things we must not forget. Forget not Athens, Rome, Corinth—centres of art and literature, yet centres of iniquity. Forget not Goethe, called "the most splendid spicimen of culture ever presented to the world"—and yet how selfish, how unworthy to woman, how impure the atmosphere of his study. Forget not Aaron Burr and Benedict Arnold, drilled in the learning of the schools! Yet what a blot their names cast upon the pages of American history! Forget not Loeb and Leopold, those young Chicago intellectuals who, for the sake of a "thrill", committed brutal murder. To make the right use of our knowledge, we need that wisdom which begins in the fear of the Lord. "The wisdom that is from above is first pure, then peaceable, gentile, and easy to be intreated, full of mercy and good fruits, without partiality, and without hypocrisy" (James 3:17).

To all who pant for knowledge, filled with a passion for truth, and to whom life is just half a thing, the vast deeps not yet cut open for them, the Bible says, "In whom (Christ) are hid all the treasures of wisdom and knowledge."

Emerson attended Longfellow's funeral. Emerson's mind, like a great cathedral gone to ruins, had left him. He looked upon the face of Longfellow, his intimate friend, and said,

> "This is a lovely soul,
> But I forget his name."

A greater tragedy than a mind in ruins is a strong mind unruled by Christ.

Consider now Christ as our only necessity for fruit-fulness and power in the kingdom of

III. The Spiritual

A sound body with a sound mind and a sound heart is a trinity of power in the exercise of which you will find life's highest greatest success. Of the third reality of that trinity of power—the spiritual—we now speak.

What is our only necessity for reaching the fulness of our possibilities, for clothing ourselves in more vigorous spiritual realities, for having power? With confidence that is absolute, with certainty that is unyielding, I point you to Jesus Christ. What food is to the body, what air is to the lungs, what numbers are to mathematics, what the all-glorious sun is to this universe, *that* and a thousand times more, Christ will be to your life.

Now, thinking of the spiritual, we must consider, first, man's first and deepest need.

What *is* man's first, greatest, deepest, most fundamental need? A Saviour? Yes. But a Saviour from what? First of all and underlying all else, a Saviour from the guilt of sin. Every man of every race has sinned. As Paul put it (Rom. 3:22) "There is no difference, for all have sinned and come short of the glory of God." There is no difference between Jew and Gentile, English and German, European and Asiatic, American and Japanese, American and African. Every man shall have to answer for his sin to the infinitely holy God who rules this universe. Therefore, all men need a Saviour—a Saviour who, by His substitutionary death, can make propitiation for our sins, and reconcile us to this holy God, and deliver us from His awful wrath and bring us out into the glorious sunlight of His favour.

Jesus is the only atoning Saviour in the universe. Jesus actually meets every man's first, greatest, deepest, most fundamental need. He alone. In all the universe there is no other religion but Christianity that even offers an atoning Saviour. Mohammedanism offers Mohammed, "The Prophet," a teacher, but not an atoning Saviour. Confucianism offers Confucius, a marvelous teacher, supposedly far ahead of his time, but not an atoning Saviour. Buddhism offers Buddha, supposedly a great teacher, but not an atoning Saviour.

The bitter cry of the race, "What shall I do with my sins?" is not hushed by some rhetorical lullaby. Jesus Christ, the hope of the race, answers that cry. He is in His glory when He gets among lost men. You never see His full stature until He gets among the fallen, the lost.

Greatness is not comfortable among the fallen, for purple does not match with sackcloth. Nor fashion, for it is too afraid its satin will be besmirched. Nor science, for while science can work miracles of transformation in the physical realm, it can work none in the heart of man. Nor art, for art retires as soon as it takes the sinner's portrait. But Jesus Christ is at home among the fallen. He is in His glory with lost souls, lost classes, lost tribes, lost races, for "the Son of man is come to seek and to save that which was lost."

What shall I do with my sins? As I turn the leaves of my Bible I find that question echoed again and again, generation after generation, age after age. Yet had Christ come into the world, it would have echoed around the globe—still unanswered and unanswerable until this very day.

"O Plato!" cried Socrates, "it may be that the gods can forgive sins, but alas! I do not see how!"

We may scour sea, land, earth, sky, for some answer to that question of the soul. We may climb the forty summits of the highest mountains and thread the labyrinthine mine. We may call to the heights of the heavens and to the depths of the sea. But there will be no answering

voice; and we are left to nurse a piteous despair until
we come to

> . . . a green hill far away,
>   Without a city wall,
>   Where our dear Lord was crucified,
>   Who died to save us all!

McArtney knew this when he wrote: "We must not
be deceived by the glitter and glamour of the material
and mechanical side of our modern civilization. Surface
things these. Autos, radios, moving pictures, airplanes,
refrigerators, all the wonderful devices of modern life
are no index to the hidden life of the soul. Immeasurable
the sadness and sorrow, the tragedy and sin of our
modern life. And you can't feed hungry souls on the saw-
dust of guesses and theories. You can't comfort broken
hearts by telling in gilded rhetoric that what they used
to believe and what their fathers used to believe, now
must be 're-interpreted' or, in plain English, abandoned. You cannot light the pathway of man across the
void of dread and darkness with the flittering phosphor-
escence of a brilliant aphorism. Now in the straits of the
soul the only message is the message of Calvary, the
story of repentance and salvation and regeneration
through faith in Christ."

Through Christ, our only necessity, is met our first
and deepest need, our stains are cleansed, our shackles
broken, our hungers satisfied, our storms quelled, our
dispositions changed, our lost things restored to the
service for which they were divinely entrusted!

When the sin question is settled, then for spiritual
achievement the leadership of Christ Himself is promised—a leadership that is comradeship as well as leadership. Following Christ's leadership unifies life, concen-
trates life, satisfies life, conserves life. It renders forever impossible such an aimless, guideless, godless, pur-

poseless life as that of Eugene de Luvois, whom Owen
Meredith describes in *Lucile*:

> Down the path of life that led nowhere he trod,
> Where his whims were his guides, and his will was his god,
> And his pastime his purpose!

Let me make this plain, straight word of appeal to
you. You need Christ in your life. You need Him as a
philosophical belief touching the origin and ground of
all finite existence, not as a mere dogma to be written
at the head of a confession of faith, not as a name to be
introduced into some liturgy which you may occasionally
employ. You need Christ as a present, personal, profound
experience. To know Him is to live and to live well. This
is victory indeed.

You see Jesus' victory over the world, the flesh, the
devil was not meant to be exceptional. It was meant to be
representative. It was to be shared by those who follow
His leadership. In tribulation, in distress, in persecution,
in famine, in nakedness, in peril, in life, in death, we are
more than conquerors through Him who acknowledges
no mastery in hostile circumstances. He who entirely
understands our nature and every situation assures us
of victory. He who knows to an ounce the weight of the
temptations that burden, will give succor. He who knows
the secret defects and secret remorse assures us that no
weapon formed against us shall prosper. He whose love
will go all lengths and stop short at no sacrifice in order
to serve our interests and the glory of God that is bound
up with them says, ''Be of good cheer, I have overcome.''

Phillips Brooks once said to an audience of Harvard
men,

''Here is the last great certainty, be sure of Christ.
By simple, loving worship, by continual obedience, by
keeping yourself pure even as he is pure, *creep* close to

him, *keep* close to him, and in the end nothing can over-throw you.''

''Nothing can overthrow you!''

That, indeed, is victory!

I am come now to our

CONCLUSION

What will you do when you return from this con-ference with that body of yours?

Where will walk the feet that make footsteps that God counts?

What sort of hands will you have?

What are you going to mean to your pastor?

What are you going to mean physically, mentally, spiritually to your church? To your friends? To the friendless? To God?

When the franchise obligation and liberty is yours, will you vote as would Christ, remembering that the ballot is the ballast of the ship of state, remembering that liberty's throne is on the ballot box and that every evil vote shakes the throne of liberty to the foundation?

Remembering that Sunday selfishness is a worse form of cancer than that which the doctors would cure with radium, will you, like Christ, like many immortals who followed in his train, be found in church on Sunday? It may be a village church, a remote mountain church, a big city church, a struggling country church. But, following Christ, you can do none other than to be there in worship, lending your voice to the hymns of praise, your ears to the Word of God, your presence and influence to the cause for which the church stands, and your hands to its tasks! It is folly to spend the acquisitive years of college in such a way as not to develop and maintain the growth of the Spirit life.

Remembering that wood and brick make a house, but only love can make a home, what will you do when mating time comes? Remembering Christ who, never having a home of his own, never sustaining the sacred relations of husband and father, founded the Christian home, enthroning love as its supreme law, will you give Him chief place?

When the voices of duty call you in times of peace, will you take your religion in a comfortable chair, or will you manifest the truth that "peace hath her victories no less renowned than war"?

Remembering that materialism, like an evil spirit, would give its cup of sorcery to youth, and beguile them from the paths of noble scholarship, the spiritually intellectual life, and the character which reaches stability, beauty, and power only when rooted in religion—what will you do?

When many atheistic pens are trying to drown the Bible the only reliable franchise of Christian hopes in infidel ink, how will you read and follow this Book which comes to us drenched in the tears of a million contritions, stained with the blood of martyrs, worn with the fingers of agony and death, expounded by the greatest intellects?

In a day when, in business, there are those who are content to maintain the shallow stream of piety that runs on Sabbath days—showing the tendency to make business one thing and religion another, each having nothing to do with the other, will you show that Christ is your only necessity to make you a business man who honors God?

With your diamond talents, will you do pewter work?

With your incandescent light abilities, will you make tallow candle light?

With your pipe organ opportunities, will you do harmonica work?

With Winchester powers, will your aim be that of the pop-gun?

With your steam shovel talents, will you dig with a spade?

Will you be guilty of embezzlement?—of embezzlement by robbing him of yourselves, of your talents, using what has been entrusted to you as if it were your own property? God forbid.

My friend, Dr. Bartholow, of Mount Vernon, New York, in his address on "The Philosopher's Stone" tells this:

"In my youth I was taught the game of chess. I have studied the game for many years and know that it is a game of exhaustless moves. More than a million have been analyzed. Steinitz, Tarrasch, Pillsbury, Larker, Capablanca, Alexhine, have made valuable contributions to the study of chess in our day, and the end is not yet.

"All who know the game, know that the checkmating of the king is the objective of the contestants. The great variety of pieces, with their multiplicity of movement in combination, makes for profundity and variety in the play. An adept at chess is able ofttimes to announce a checkmate of an opponent's king in a certain number of moves. Obviously this requires a close and comprehensive knowledge of all the moves possible by the various pieces under all conditions. Should a player announce a checkmate in four moves, it would mean that his opponent had no possible way of escape, no matter what combination he should form with his own pieces.

"Years ago from a great chess player of Cincinnati we learned that in the early part of the last century an artist who was a great chess player painted a picture of a chess game. The players were a young man and Satan. The young man manipulated the white pieces; Satan the black pieces. The issue of the game was this: should the young man win, he was to be forever free from the power of evil; should the devil win, the young man was to be his slave forever. The artist evidently believed in the supreme power of evil, for his picture presented the devil as victor.

"In the conception of the artist, the devil had just moved his queen and had announced a checkmate in four moves. The young man's hand hovered over his rook; his face paled with amazement. There was no hope. The devil wins! He was to be a slave forever!

"For years this picture hung in a great art gallery. Chess players from all over the world viewed the picture. They acquiesced in the thought of the artist. The devil wins! After several years a chess doubter arose; he saw and studied this picture, became convinced that there was but one chess player upon the earth who could give him assurance that the artist of this picture was right in his conception of the winner. The chess player was the aged Paul Morphy, a resident of New Orleans, La. Morphy was a supreme master of chess in his day, an undefeated champion. He had quit the game because of mental strain. A scheme was arranged by our chess doubter through which Morphy was brought to Cincinnati and to a view of the chess picture.

"On beholding the picture two mighty impulses arose in the old master's mind, the first, that which leads a brave man to take the part of the under dog; the second, that which resents the passing of a crown of supremacy which had not been challenged.

"Morphy stood before the picture, five minutes, ten minutes, twenty minutes, thirty minutes. He was all concentration; he lifted and lowered his hands as, in imagination, he made and eliminated moves. Suddenly his hand paused, his eyes burned with the vision of an unthought-of combination. Suddenly he shouted, 'Young man, make that move. That's the move!'

"To the amazement of all, the old master, *the supreme chess personality,* had discovered a combination that the creating artist had not considered. The young man defeated the devil. The *master* personality had come!''

Hasten, ye young hearts, to make, under the Master's bidding, your campus a camp of Christians responding sacrificially to the marching orders of His kingdom's great advance—make that move!

Remembering that material things are rightly handled only when they are instruments of God's will, honor the Lord with a definite portion of your income. Make that move!

Make the move that shows you have the holy boldness to choose intangible values. Make that move!

Turn your backs upon the evil or unworthy in your own careers and press toward the best things, toward the heights of happiness, toward the triumphs of service. That's the move!

Hasten, young hearts, under the urge of His call, to your part in making literature, learning, government, religion, business, captives marching in Christ's triumphal procession up the hill of time. That's the move!

Make the move that would let your close companion, your campus, your home, your community, your church, your teachers, your pastor, know that for power and consecration in the physical, mental, and spiritual realms, you swear anew your fidelity! That's the move!

Show that, for common humanity, you are willing to give your disinterested love, your deepest sympathy, the talents God has given you, the right and reasonable portion of your time, your ripest thoughts, your eyes to see golden opportunities, your ears to catch the Macedonian call, your feet to run on the king's errands, your hands to minister to the needy, your voice to tell the wondrous story, your money to send the message to earth's remotest people! That's the move!

Make the move that, under Christ, will make you walk

like an archangel down life's plain common way. That's the move!

Make the move that will show those who sell their future for a mess of pottage that you will know how, under His prompting, to choose the wheat from the chaff! That's the move!

Make the move that would take you out of the sidelines and put you in the game for God with a fine, full measure of consecration, of capacity for self-sacrifice. Make the move now! Then you will find earth the threshold of heaven! And your joy such that no man or circumstance can take it from you.

Chapter 4

THE TREASURES OF DARKNESS

I will give thee the treasures of darkness (Isaiah 45:3).
He discovereth deep things out of darkness (Job 12:22).

Though God has assured us that there are treasures in the darkness and, for us, discovers deep things out of the darkness,

I. DARKNESS IS DREADED

Humanity now, even as in ages past, from childhood to old age, seems to dread darkness. "Afraid of the dark" seems to be true with many—true in great measure in childhood, true in lesser measure in youth, true also in old age. Misgivings smite the mind when night comes. Men think of darkness as the time when beasts prowl, when wild things of the jungle come forth, when many evil designs of man come to fruitage. Darkness—the time when brutal men and abandoned women haunt the deep shadows. Darkness—the time when base sons and wanton daughters of Belial, who love darkness rather than light because their deeds are evil, prey upon the helpless sleeper and upon the hapless wayfarer.

Hamlet expressed the universal dread of darkness in the words,

'Tis now the very witching time of night,
When churchyards yawn, and hell itself breathes out

Contagion to this world: now could I drink hot blood,
And do such bitter business as the day
Would quake to look on.

And because man through ages has seemed to dread darkness, he has had the torch, candle, lamp, electric light, and lighthouse.

Hill, in agreement with Shakespeare, says,

Treacherous darkness! Thou lendest thy ready veil to every treason, and teeming mischiefs thrive beneath thy shades.

Spencer emphasizes the same thing,

Under thy black mantle there hidden lie, light shunning theft,
And traitorous intent, abhorred, bloodshed,
And vile felony, shameful deceit,
And danger imminent, foul horror,
And eke hellish dreariment.

Vice and misery, to prowl, or to moan like night birds are abroad.

A dread storm is made more dreadful if it comes in the darkness of night.

A conflagration that lights a city and eats its destructive way is made terrible if it comes in the darkness of the night.

An earthquake has its horrors intensified and multiplied if it comes, swallowing up houses and cities, in the night.

War, with its whining bullets and booming cannon, poison gas and thirsty swords, is made more terrible when Mars walks with bloody boots in the darkness of the night.

"He hath set me in dark places, as they be dead of old" (Lamentations 3:6). Thus Jeremiah expresses man's dread of darkness.

"For the dark places of the earth are full of the *habitations of cruelty*" (Psalm 74:20). In these striking words the Psalmist expresses the same truth.

"In the dark they dig through houses, which they had

marked for themselves in the daytime: they *know not
the light*" (Job 24:16). So Job declares how evil men
carry out their evil designs under the black mantle of
night.

"And he went the way to her house, In the twilight, in
the evening, *in the black and dark night*" (Proverbs 7:8,
9). In these striking words Solomon shows how shameful deceit works under cover of the darkness.

"The land of darkness is *the grave*" (Job 10:21). In
this pungent sentence Job speaks again of man's inward
revulsion toward darkness.

"An *horror* of great darknes fell upon him" (Genesis
15:12). Brief meditation on this sentence shows that to
Abraham there were occasions when darkness was full
of horror.

"Hath reserved in everlasting chains under darkness"
(Jude 6).

These and many other verses show us that man has
dreaded darkness and oft has used it as a symbol of the
pestilence, plague, calamity, and death. A symbol of
ignorance, tyranny, and sinfulness in darkness—so men
have said. One man wrote, "Darkness is the outlaw's
day." And with him many agree.

But darkness has its treasures.

This Young meant to show when he said,

Darkness has **divinity** for me. It strikes thought inward; it drives
back the soul to settle on herself, our point supreme. There lies
our theater. There sits our judge. Darkness the curtain drops o'er
life's dull scene. 'Tis the **kind hand of Providence** stretched out 'twixt
man and vanity. 'Tis reason's reign, and virture's, too. These tutelary
shades are man's asylum from the tainted throng. Night is the
good man's friend and guardian, too.

Of this, of the *treasures* of the darkness, May was
thinking when he wrote,

Night's silent reign hath robbed the world of light, to lend, in
lieu, a greater benefit.

And the blest old Book speaks of the treasures of the darkness. And the darkness has its treasures, as saith the Book of books. The Word of the Lord is full of song, rising from the hearts of those whose night-time has been sweet through their communion with the Heavenly Father. Here follows a chorus of confirmation showing forth in every word and sentence the treasures the darkness possesses,

Thou hast visited me in the night (Psalm 17:3).
In the night his song shall be with me (Psalm 42:8).
At midnight I will rise to give thanks (Psalm 119:62).
At midnight Paul and Silas prayed and sang praises (Acts 16:25).

Even amid the cold pressure of darkness they found treasures in the darkness, even as one finds pearls in dark recesses of the ocean bed, even as one finds silver and gold in the dark bowels of the earth.

But, what are the treasures of darkness? Let us see. Let us make assertion that

II. DARKNESS SYMBOLIZES SIN FOR US

They meet with darkness in the daytime (Job 5:14).

Evil-doers do. *All* evil-doers do.

For sin, even in noonday brightness, is darkness. Sin is darkness *now*. Sin always has been darkness. Sin always will be darkness. Everywhere and all the time sin is that black darkness that invests man's whole moral being, Sin is that black thing that was in existence before the Bible. It is the dread and deadly disease that was felt before the remedy was known. It is the black and terrible riddle that has perplexed human thought before the answer was proclaimed. It is life's inexorable and most dreadful curse!

Yes, sin is the black adder that strikes in the dark, the black bloodthirsty panther that springs without warning and crushes without mercy, the black Numidian lion seeking whom it may devour, the black poison that pollutes the stream of life.

And there are three things the true Christian desires in respect to sin! He desires justification that sin may not condemn. He desires sanctification that sin may not reign. He desires glorification that sin may not be.

Sin, everywhere and always, is darkness in the daytime. The drunkard is walking in midnight at noonday, meeting with darkness in the daytime. The gambler is walking in black night at noonday. The adulterer walks night's black shadows at noonday. The harlot walks in darkness even when the sunshine is round about her, meeting with darkness in the daytime. The liar walks in darkness in the daytime. The cheat, the fraud, walks in the darkness in noontime. All these and all evil-doers meet with darkness in the daytime. How true it is that "the way of the wicked is as darkness: they know not" (Proverbs 4:19).

But somebody asks, "Wherein is there any treasure in the darkness in respect to sin?"

Well, let me ask, is it not a priceless thing to know that darkness symbolizes sin and thus warns us against yielding to sin? Is not this treasure indeed? I look down into the dark of a dread abyss, and it speaks to me of the darkness of the pathless depths and treacherous abysses of sin. I look into the darkness of caverns, and there the exitless darkness and the flit and flap of black bats' wings warn me against that terrible outer darkness where the associates of eternity are the damned. I look into the darkness of the loathsome and festering alley, and it warns me of the darkness of iniquity.

I would thank any one, were I an engineer, if he would show me a symbol telling that the bridge was down and the flood was raging. I would be thankful to any one if he gave me a sign in the midst of mine enemies that the food I was about to eat was full of deadly fever germs. Were I a pilgrim in a strange land, I would thank any one who gave me a sign whereby I should know that the water I was about to drink was contaminated. Were I a sea captain, I would consider as treasure the lighthouse, though grim and black, that warned me away from the rocky coast. Lighthouses are not placed on our rocky shores for adornment, but to warn mariners of a dangerous point. Buoys are black and uncomely, but they tell us where the rocks are.

One time on the Texas prairie, I came upon a rattler. I heard a buzz that got the attention of my ears and eyes more quickly than the New York Symphony orchestra would have gotten it—a buzz that *held* my attention more intensely than the eloquence of Demosthenes or Bryan would have held it—more than the singing of Frieda Hempel, or the playing of Beethoven. That rattlesnake's rattle was hideous, but it gave timely warning of something more dreadful. When I thought of his poisonous fangs, so dangerously ready, I was glad for the buzz of his rattles.

Think of the skull and cross-bones. This hideous symbol is not pretty to look at, but it is a *valuable* sign which warns of deadly poison and of death through poison! Murderous those who change the warning label into something meaningless. So one great treasure of the darkness is that *in what it symbolizes* as to sin it is valuable. The darkness is a diamond district we may all explore—a diamond mine in which we find treasures for life, treasures for eternity!

Think of crepe on the door knob. I never like to see it. Yet it is a treasure in that it symbolizes that death has come and that, because death has come, it is a time for sympathy, prayer, and sober thought. Paul asked, "Am I therefore become your enemy, because I tell you the truth?" (Galatians 4:16). Would you become the enemy of the night because it symbolizes the darkness of sin? Would you think it wiser for the mariner to take the clapper out of the bell that floats and tolls above a shoal on which the ship will be wrecked if it strikes? Would it be wise to put out the lighthouse lamps, and then think that you had abolished the reef? Does the signalman with the red flag *make* the danger that he warns of? Is it not like Ahab in his hatred of Micaiah to hate the message that comes to you?

God has given us "the treasures of the darkness" and "discovered deep things out of the darkness" for us in that from horizon to horizon, in cellar and in attic where darkness dwells he has symbolized the black darkness of sin and the horrible outer darkness where there is weeping, wailing and gnashing of teeth.

But consider also that darkness puts before us

III. THE TREASURES OF REVELATION

The darkness hides from man's sight.

The darkness never hides from God's sight. Midnight is as the noonday to Him. "The darkness and the light are both alike to thee" (Psalm 139:12).

But one of the treasures of the darkness is what it reveals. Darkness hides the near on which we dwell so much. Darkness reveals the far on which we dwell but little. Darkness may hide the river flowing toward the sea, but it reveals the Milky Way across the sky. Darkness may hide the rose bush at our feet, but not the infinite meadows of heaven. It may hide the ocean from our sight where man's ships go, but it reveals the ocean of the sky where the stars, like golden yachts at anchor, shine steadily.

The darkness reveals the stars.

Immanuel Kant, the great philosopher, said, "The two grandest things in nature are the starry heavens as midnight and the conscience in the human breast."

Victor Hugo, the great writer, wrote, "The three

grandest things—the ocean, the sky, the interior of the human soul.''

Napoleon, the great soldier, declared, ''I find in the stars all the proof I want of the existence of God.''

Marvelous it is how much the Bible says about the stars—the stars which we would not see but for the darkness.

Does it wish to declare that God is entitled to worship? ''Praise him, all ye stars of light'' (Psalm 148:3).

Does it wish to show what a defense God is to His people? ''The stars in their courses fought against Sisera'' (Judges 5:20).

Does it wish to express inconceivable number? ''As the stars of heaven for multitude'' (Deuteronomy 1:10).

Does it wish to express God's absolute holiness? ''Behold, . . . the stars are not pure in his sight'' (Job 25:5).

Does it wish to set forth God's omniscience? ''He telleth the number of the stars; he calleth them all by their names'' (Psalm 147:4).

Does it wish to rebuke man's arrogance? ''Though thou set thy nest among the stars, thence will I bring thee down'' (Obadiah 4).

Does it wish to announce God's sure victory? ''I will exalt my throne above the stars'' (Isaiah 14:13).

Does it wish to speak of the doom of the impenitent? It calls them ''wandering stars, to whom is reserved the blackness of darkness for ever'' (Jude 13).

Does it wish to depict the awfulness of the last day? ''The stars shall fall from heaven'' (Matthew 24:29).

Does it wish to show forth the glory of the godly? They ''shall shine . . . as the stars for ever and ever'' (Daniel 12:3).

Does it wish to assure us of the ultimate triumph of Christ? ''The sun and the moon and the stars shall be put under his feet.''

What treasures in the darkness when we remember

that it reveals the stars, and in revealing the stars reveals a God of order, a God, our God, who knows the schedule of the comets; a God, our father's God, who commands the rising and setting suns; a God, our omnipotent God, who put the satellites in reverse order in Uranus!

What treasures in the darkness when we know that in revealing the stars it thus speaks of Jesus, the Bright and Morning Star, who said, "I am the light of the world."

What treasures in the darkness when we know that it was in the three hours of darkness on the Cross Jesus was forsaken of God that we might not be forsaken!

Astronomer's have learned much about the sun from the darkness of the eclipse. When the shadow shoots off the central light, they can see the corona, the crown of light flashing far into space on every side. They could not see it before because there was too much light. The darkness revealed its glory and crowned the sun, just as the shadow of sorrow shows us the shining glory of faith and sets a crown on Christian life.

"The night has a thousand eyes!" This statement does not disparage the day. In the day one sees most clearly, in the night one sees the farthest. In the day one thinks the brightest thoughts, in the night one thinks the deepest thoughts. In the day we think the thoughts of men. In the darkness of the night we, if spiritually minded, have many thoughts of God. "In the night watches I will meditate on thee." Thus the darkness reveals God to us. "When I sit in darkness, the Lord shall be a light unto me" (Micah 7:8). If it be night in the arctic circle, if it be night amid the wastes of snow and ice and loneliness, if it be night in the temperate zone amid busy nations, if it be the darkness of the tropics heavy with the fragrance of magnolia, if it be

darkness in the dungeon for righteousness' sake, God
is nigh. And He will be a light. For

"He made darkness his secret place; his pavilion
round about him were dark waters and thick clouds"
(Psalm 18:11).

All that the stars reveal to us we owe to the darkness
which reveals the stars. If the twenty-four hours were
all daylight, we would be bereft of the joys the stars
give us. If we lived in a world that was all day, we would
never see the stars that gem the brow of night.

We must remember also that

IV. DARKNESS DEVELOPS

Darkness has its blessed ministry and uses as well as
the sunlight. God has made a world in which frost is
needed as well as sunshine; a world in which storm is
needed to make the trees take deeper root; a world in
which suffering and sorrows have treasures of their own
to bring to the spirit. God's highest revelation was in
Jesus Christ who passed through the darkness of Calvary—His naked body quivering and blood-splotched
against the darkness. And God is more concerned for
our character than for our comfort. He is more concerned
for our moral purity than for our physical immunity.
He is more concerned for our freedom from poison of
evil than for our freedom from danger. Therefore, He
puts us in the dark of tribulation oftentimes. He puts
us in the dark in the prison house of pain. The seed must
first be in the dark of the ground before it comes to the
plant that makes the fruit. The foundation must first
be placed in the ground ere it can hold the great sky-
scraper.

Souls are like photograph plates. Photographic plates
are sensitive. So God has made our souls like photographic plates prepared and sensitive to receive the
beauty and the grace which He wishes to print on them.

But it takes the dark room to bring out what is there. Just as plates are all alike, until you take them into the dark and develop them, so people are very much alike until God takes them into this dark room of sorrow, disappointment, and trial. It is the discipline of the darkness of the dark room that brings out the difference.

God takes John Milton into the dark room of blindness, and the wonderful thing that develops is the world's greatest epic, *Paradise Lost,* and one of the great songs of the world, *Paradise Regained.*

God takes John Bunyan into the dark room of the Bedford prison and persecution. And what develops there is the wonderful picture of the *The Pilgrim's Progress,* a book which broke out of that jail and is now walking many highways, traveling many bypaths, knocking at many doors, and speaking to many people in their mother tongue.

God takes John the apostle into the dark room of exile in Patmos, and wonderful pictures of the city of God and mighty music of the triumph of Christ develop.

God takes Fanny Crosby into the dark room of blindness. But over the walls of her prison house of darkness over eight thousand songs arise to circle the world.

So some people go into God's darkness, and He gives them what the Bible calls "the treasures of darkness." Sorrow brings out what sunshine had printed on their souls, and they come out of the shadows and the darkness and the sorrow with something of the likeness of Christ. So, in many ways we learn that the darkness is the servant of the light!

Helen Keller said, "Out of the night of my individual blindness has come a call—the urge of others' need. It is as persistent as the love note which the mother birds hear when their nestlings are in trouble. And I know it will never cease until the wall of darkness has been broken down for my one hundred thousand companions in darkness.'' Of what is she speaking? Of the treasures she found in the darkness!

The Lord hath said that he would dwell in the thick darkness (II Chronicles 6:1).

> And many a rapturous minstrel,
>   Among those sons of light,
> Will say of his sweetest music,
>   'I learned it in the night.'
>
> And many a rolling anthem,
>   That fills the Father's home,
> Sobbed out its first rehearsal,
>   In the shade of a darkened room.

God gives a treasure in the darkness by revealing

V. BLESSINGS IN THE BLACK

"The heaven was black with clouds" (I Kings 18:45). But there were blessings in the black, blessings in the heavens dark with clouds. For a long, long time—over three years in Ahab's reign—there had been no rain. But after the rain the brooks broke their silence, the rivers were no longer dumb, the trees clapped their hands for joy, the fields and meadows rejoiced, nature spread her carpets of green and hung her curtains of green. Flocks and herds were saved from death. Similarly so in life, our lives are black with sorrows and defeats and trials and bereavements. But there are many spiritual blessings in the black if only we have eyes to see, ears to hear and hands to receive.

With Jesus and His teachings and His miracle it was all sunlight. Joy was in all His parables. Joy of women finding lost coins; joy of shepherds finding lost sheep; joy of fathers having lost sons come home again. So much joy that the frozen-hearted Pharisee found fault with Jesus and His disciples. Then one day Jesus told the disciples about the other things that were coming.

He showed them the *black* in the picture—the CROSS and DEATH. And Peter protested that this must never be. He, too, like many others, did not like the black because he did not know the black was to become gold.

But the black day came. The betrayal. The arrest. The spit in the face. The scourge. The mocking. The crown of thorns. The Cross. The three hours of darkness. The death. The burial. It seemed to them all black. His throne had disappeared in a tomb. His kingdom had shrunk to the narrow dimensions of a grave. Their heavens were black with clouds. Then at last they saw and understood, for the wound, the Cross and the crown of thorns shone out in golden glory. They "beheld his glory" as they had never seen it or imagined it. They learned on the resurrection morning the blessings there are in the black, in the darkness!

Black shadows will fall on your road. Do not be afraid of them. Do not be afraid of the black. Remember that when God lays on the black, He is preparing for the gold, without which life misses its perfect beauty. "When he has tried me, I shall come forth as gold" (Job 23:10). When the disciples were looking forward to the Cross, it was a terrible thing. They couldn't bear to think of it. But when they got to the other side of that black thing dripping with blood, it was wonderful and beautiful, and they could talk of nothing else. "When all the forces of darkness seemed to be triumphant, then in reality the Son of God won His greatest victory, and the Cross has become the tree which has sweetened all the bitter waters of the world."

A bit of verse by a poet says the same thing,

> Rose purple and a silvery gray
> Is that cloud, the cloud which looked so black.
> Evening brightens all today,
> Looking back.

And another, speaking of the blackness of death, that dark door which awaits us all, showing that there is blessing in the black,

> The face of death is towards the sun of life,
> Its shadow darkens earth.

There is a blessing in the black when the darkness is seen from the right side. The pillar of cloud was a cloud of darkness to the Egyptians, but it gave a light to the Israelites. To the Christian, the door of death, black and dark as it may be, will give light to the redeemed. Dickens, when a neglected little boy, working in a blacking factory, went into a coffee house in St. Martin's lane. The first time he looked up from his chair he saw two words on the glass door that set him all a-tremble. He had not noticed them coming in. The awful words were *Moor Eeffoc*. But he was looking at those words with fear in his heart because he was seeing them from the wrong view. When he got outside and looked in he saw the dreadful words *Moor Eeffoc* change to the inviting words *Coffee Room*.

Moor Eeffoc, No. But *Coffee Room*—when seen and read as they were meant to be seen and read. Just as "Moor Eeffoc" turned out to be only "Coffee Room," so the doors which spell out "Trial," "Disappointment," "Tears," "Duty," "Sorrow," and even "Death," when we see the blessing in the black will spell out to us *"Blessing"* and "God-is-love." This is only another way of saying that God will give us the treasures of the darkness and reveal to us deep things out of the darkness.

> Where did you get your roses child?
> "I made them in this little room."
> Your window happy with the dawn?
> "No, sir; in fearful gloom."

What gave your roses color then?
  "My blood, sir, as I bent my head."
Your cheek is cold and lifeless now?
  "No, sir; that's my heart that bled."

One white rose in the basket child?
  "Yes, sir, it crowns the whole."
What is it, fragile, soft and white?
  "I think it is my soul."

Beauty came in the dark. Beauty came with bleeding! And so also came the blessing. Treasures of darkness. Deep things discovered out of the darkness!

They tell me I must bruise
  The rose's leaf,
Ere I can reap and use
  The fragrance brief.

They tell me I must break
  The skylark's heart
Ere her song will make
  The silence start.

They tell me love must bleed,
  And friendship weep,
Ere in my deepest need
  I touch that deep.

Must it be always so
  With precious things?
Must they be bruised and go
  With beaten wings?

Ah, yes! By crushing days,
  By caging nights, by scar
Of thorns and stony ways
  Those blessings are.

"By caging nights . . . those blessings are." Just our text dressed in another language-garment!

Dickens unfolds this truth in *David Copperfield*. Mrs.

Gummidge is the most self-centered, ill-content, cross-grained woman in Yarmouth. Then comes the angel of sorrow, with black and heavy wings. All those around her are plunged in the shadow of a terrible calamity. And, in ministering to them, the whole life and character of Mrs. Gummidge was transfigured.

> If sorrow never claimed our heart;
> And every wish were granted,
> Patience would die, and hope depart,
> Life would be disconsolate!

Late in the last century a student graduated from the Boston University school of theology. The first five years in ministry found him as a man of growing power. Then severe sickness left him a confirmed invalid. Slowly the tide of suffering arose along the shores of his body. One leg was amputated; one leg withered; one eye failed. Then the other eye failed, leaving him in darkness forever—joints stiffened, ossified. His spinal column hardened. Then he had left only one hand and one arm. Out of this prolonged Gethsemane came a book, *God's White Throne*, a cleverly-reasoned article proving the absolute goodness of God.

"When he has tried me, I shall come forth as gold." The fire of the furnace and the smoke of the flames show how God brings deep things out of the darkness, rich treasures out of darkness.

Authorities tell us that the potter never sees his clay take on rich shades of silver, or red, or cream, or brown, or yellow, until after the darkness and the burning of the furnace. These colors come after the burning and darkness. The clay is beautiful after the burning and darkness. The vase is made possible after the burning and darkness. After the burning and darkness, we own a purity that sees God. After the burning and darkness, we have a wisdom that knows God. After the burning and blackness, our weakness is coined into strength and we lean upon God. After the burning and blackness, our faith is no longer a flickering flame, but an eye set in the soul through which we behold the face of God. If the burning hurts and the darkness brings gloom, as it always does, it is only a prophecy of the strength which will be ushered into life. When the little girl told her music teacher that it hurt her fingers to practice on the piano, the teacher answered, ''I know it hurts them, but it *strengthens* them, too.'' Then the child packed the philosophy of the ages in her reply, ''Teacher, it seems that everything which strengthens, hurts.''

How wide-lying and universal is the law of life! Where did the bravest man and purest women you know get their whitened characters? Did they not get them as the clay gets its beauty—after the darkness and the burning of the furnace? Where did your mother get that look which, as you think, would add dignity to an angel's face? Already God has written the answer—after the darkness and the burning. Where did Savonarola get his eloquence? In the darkness and burning of the furnace wherein God revealed deep things to him. Where did Stradivari get his violins? Where did Titian get his color? Where did Angelo get his marbles? Where did Mozart get his music, Chatterton his poetry, Palissy his enamel, and Jeremiah his sermon? They got them where the clay gets its glory and its shimmer—in the darkness and in the burning. Truly they can testify that God kept his promise, who said, ''I will give thee the treasures of darkness.''

I have read the life story of Katie Powers who died at a home for incurables in Cleveland. When her spirit left its twisted, mis-shapen body, strong men told their strength in tears. Katie was a bright, happy girl, but disease did all in its power to rob life of its winsome-ness for her. In the flush of young womanhood, inflammatory rheumatism left her unable to walk. But when God made this girl out of the dust of the earth, he did not forget to slip some of the dust of character-gold in her soul. Deprived of bodily power, she said, "But think how much I have left." Then her arms stiffened. And her fingers drew up like claws. And her jaw became so rigid that it would have been impossible for her to eat but for the fact that her teeth were extracted to permit the introduction of food. And her vision also forsook her, leaving only a little sight in one eye. For years she lay huddled up in an invalid's chair. She could see a little; she could move her arms a little; but that was all!

And what did she do? She became a painter. She would lie there and paint sunny bits of water color. And the pictures did not reveal, as Shannon testifies, the slightest hint of the sufferer in the background. They laughed with sunshine and blushed with hope. People never thought of pitying her, so they simply loved her. She carried not only her burdens, but the burdens of others also. "Whenever I get blue," said a neighbor, "I go in and see Katie; she always cheers me up." "No life ever seemed to be so truly Christian," said one. "It makes you believe in God," said another. And when her beautiful spirit went up to receive the kiss of God, many a heart in that city was draped in sorrow, while the angels wreathed her "in a smile of white." The pathos and inspiration of it all is, though helpless herself, this pure, white martyr maid of pain helped others. After the darkness; after she found the treasures of darkness; after God revealed to her deep things out of the darkness, she helped others.

But the darkness has for us the treasures of

VI. THE VISIONS OF THE NIGHT

The visions of the night (Job 4:13).

The day has its visions—visions of earthly objects, the flowers, the trees, the hills and the mountains. The night also has its visions—visions of heavenly objects, the moon, the stars and countless other radiant orbs. Only at night are these celestial bodies visible to us.

Darkness is the time for vision. What treasures, therefore, in darkness! When a motion picture is about to be shown to the audience, the house is darkened so that one may see the movements of the people on the screen. There in the dark house we settle back comfortably and note the glories of the landscape, the distant mountains, the dash of the cataract, and the sheen of the moon on the still lake—all this in the darkness. There in the darkness we can smile at the comedy. In the darkness we weep at the tragedy. In the darkness we can be enchanted at the beauty of the world that passes before us. In the darkness we can see distant scenes. So, too, God sometimes darkens our place on earth, puts out this light and that light, and then before our souls in the darkness, reveals the splendors of heaven.

Go to California. Go up the Pacific, out through the Golden Gate, northward along the coast of California. Or go to old Colon harbor on the Atlantic side. Night, night with its *darkness,* will come. Ask the chief officer of your ship if you may go to the pilot's house. If the captain will let you, you will be led up a narrow stairway *in pitch darkness*. You will step into a little room. There will be a sharp click of an electric button. A flood of light. A man leaning over a wheel like a spider over a web. Another man in uniform will speak to you. Then there will be another click. And then—again—darkness. Then you will see what you could not have seen had the pilot house not been made dark. The red light out in the distance marks a submerged ledge running from the shore far out into the channel. That alternate flash of red and white is a lighthouse. Those two colored lights, one red and the other green, one glowing like a gorgeous ruby, the other shining like a brilliant emerald, are lights on a tug. That necklace of hugh, white pearls stretched out behind is made up of lanterns on the tug's row of barges. But no one can see those lights when the room blazes with light. The officer, if you ask an explanation of the dark pilot house, will say to you, "You see, we have to *keep it dark* here, or we cannot see the light outside."

Fine! I am glad he told us that. For it helps me to say what I wish to my friend and fellow voyager who is in the darkness of the sick room. And it also helps me say what I want out of a heart that would do you good and not evil to those of you shut in from the light and music and gaiety of the world. And to you sitting in the darkness of a death-room where your loved ones lie. And to you who are now passing through financial darkness. And to you who are passing through the darkness of poverty. And to you who are sitting in the deep darkness of adversity. And to you who are in the midnight blackness of misfortune. And to you who dwell in the darkness of misrepresentation. And to you who are in the dark midnight of disgrace. And to you who are in the darkness of physical distress. And to you in the darkness of a nervous breakdown. And to you in the darkness of domestic trouble.

From your dark room look out of the window toward the skyline. You will see some faint lights in the darkness. These lights you could not have noticed in the glare. Be patient. Christ said, "The people which sat in darkness saw a great light." It was the light of the glory of God in the face of Christ Jesus. It was, even as now, the light from the throne.*

Folks can almost love the darkness of their pilot house if they know the pilot is near! Look out the window from your darkened room and pray:

> Jesus, Saviour, pilot me
> Over life's tempestuous sea:
> Unknown waves before me roll,
> Hiding rocks and treach'rous shoal;
> Chart and compass come from thee,
> Jesus, Saviour, pilot me.
>
> As a mother stills her child,
> Thou canst hush the ocean wild;
> Boist'rous waves obey Thy will
> When Thou say'st to them 'Be still!'
> Wondrous Sovereign of the sea,
> Jesus, Saviour, pilot me.
>
> When at last I near the shore,
> And the fearful breakers roar
> 'Twixt me and the peaceful rest,
> Then, while leaning on Thy breast,
> May I hear Thee say to me,
> 'Fear not, I will pilot thee.'

And, as you pray, forget not that

> The wings of God are wide and cast a shadow
> Wider than condor's wings or the albatross;
> Their shadow is very dark, as dark as midnight,
> Their shadow is dark as the shadow of the Cross.
>
> Yet under them shalt thou trust. Evil shall go by thee
> Safe in the darkness under thy God's wide wings;
> Though thou hear mountains moving and arrows are flying,
> Thou shalt be still as a child whose mother sings.
>
> Far outside in the light are thy joy and sorrow;
> Forget, forget the pleasant things thou hast left,
> Out from thy mind anxiety and hunger,
> Hope that was long deferred and love bereft.

*This illustration from Purvis.

Have now no fear of the darkness that enfolds thee,
  God's wings are spread as an eagle's over her nest.
The wings of God are wide and safe for hiding,
  There in the darkness shall thy soul find rest.

I will give thee the treasures of darkness (Isaiah 45:3).
He discovereth deep things out of darkness (Job 12:22).

Chapter 5

IT IS FINISHED

It is finished (John 19:30).

Jesus, on Golgotha, looked up and down.

He looked up to God and thought of His having glorified His name, having finished the work that God gave him to do.

He looked down to men and thought of the saving power which His Cross was to exert over millions of the human family.

And it was a moment of the most intense joy—His last pang endured, His last service rendered, His vicarious work completed.

And He said, "It is finished." That expression is the authoritative chronicle of sacrificial redemption. That is the meaning of the text, and the only meaning. Let us fasten the microscopes of spiritual scrutiny and the telescopes of spiritual observation upon this text— one of the greatest in all the Bible—and pray that, in what we shall say, we shall not spoil God's fair lilies with man's mean paint!

I. A Cry of Joy, of Supreme Satisfaction, over a Finished Work

The more difficult and prolonged any task is, the greater is the satisfaction in finishing it. Every one who has aimed at the best, knows what it means, after

accomplishing anything on which a great deal of labor
has been bestowed or the accomplishment of which has
been delayed, to be able to say, "There, it is finished
at last!"

As Gray—after finishing his elegy, every line of
which is like a jewel falling down a golden stairway.
As Virgil—after finishing his "Aeneid," all of which
is masterful. As Palissy—after working sixteen years,
amid poverty and trial, in toil and suffering, to find
the secret of white enamel. As Goodyear—after working
eleven years for the secret of vulcanizing rubber, no
one believing in him but his wife. As Morse—when, amid
the adverse criticisms of the press and the jeers of con-
gress, the metallic lips of his telegraph instrument
startled the world with the words, "What hath God
wrought?" As Cyrus Field—when, after thirty dif-
ferent attempts covering a period of ten years, during
which time his cable was denounced as a mad freak of
stubborn ignorance, he put it into the ocean bed and
it began to quiver with the news of the world. As Mc-
Cormick—when, amid jeers and ridicule that tried his
soul as fire, he got his reaper finished—a machine that
moved all the nations of the world out of the bread line.
As Galileo—when he finished the telescope which
brought the worlds and stars nearer to man's eye. As
Bell—when, after being called a mad man at the Cen-
tennial Exposition in 1876, transmitted the human voice
across the continent by means of wires. As the builder
of Taj Mahal— when, after twenty thousand men worked
on it for twenty years, was able to say, "It is finished!"
As Solomon—when, after one hundred and eighty thousand folks had worked on it for seven and one-half years,
he could say, "The glorious temple is finished!"

And others!

In the more signal efforts of human genius and energy,
there is a satisfaction in final achievement which warms

even spectators to admiration and praise across the space of hundreds of years.

What must it be to the poet, after equipping himself by the labors of a lifetime, with the stores of knowledge and the skill required in the use of language for the composition of a "Divine Comedy" or a "Paradise Lost," and after wearing himself lean for many years at the task, to be able, penning the last line, to say with satisfaction, "It is finished!"

What must it have been to Columbus, after he had worn his life out in seeking the patronage necessary for his undertaking, and having endured the perils of voyaging across uncharted seas and among mutinous mariners, to see, at last, the sunlight on the peak of Darien—which light informed him that his dream was true and his life work accomplished?

When we read how William Wilberforce, the champion of slave emancipation, heard, on his death-bed, that the British Legislature had agreed to the expenditure necessary to secure the object to which he had sacrificed his life,—what heart can refuse its sympathetic joy, as it thinks of him expiring with the shouts of e-mancipated millions in his ears?

These are but feeble and faint suggestions of that which Christ saw, fallen behind, His task accomplished, as He cried, "It is finished!" Over His teaching, He had satisfaction—wonderful satisfaction. Over His life, He had satisfaction—sweet satisfaction. Over His miracles, He had satisfaction—comforting satisfaction.

But the satisfaction of these could not compare with the satisfaction which was His, when, amid the low shame and sore torment of the Cross, He cried with inarticulate loud voice and then, in an articulate voice saying, "It is finished!" Because He had something in His mind greater than His teachings. Greater than

His life itself. Greater than His miracles. Which brings us to the question—*what* was finished?

We answer that in part when we say

II. THAT CRY—"IT IS FINISHED"—WAS A DEATH-KNELL

A death-blow? Yes. A death-knell? Yes. But a death-blow to what? A death-blow—a finishing of the dispensation of types and symbols.

Adam was a type of Christ because he came directly from God.

Melchisedek was a type of Christ because he was without beginning, without end.

Isaac was a type of Christ because he was offered on the altar of sacrifice.

Moses was a type of Christ because he was a great emancipator.

Joseph was a type of Christ in that he was despised by his brethren.

Solomon—because of the affluence of his reign.

Joshua—because of his victorious conquests.

Samson—because he carried off the gates of impossibility.

Jonah was a type of Christ because he was thrown into the midst of the sea to save others from distress.

All these were types of Christ in some especial application. Noah's ark, the rent veil, the ark of the covenant, the mercy seat, the brazen altar, the golden altar, the golden candle stick, the brazen laver, the manna, the brazen serpent, the rock of Horeb, the cities of refuge, the tree of life—*all,* in some sense, types of Christ and are so treated in the Scriptures!

So the high priest of the Jews, in the performance of every function appertaining to his sacerdotal office, was a type of Christ our High Priest—especially and pre-eminently so when on the great annual Day of

Atonement he went into the Holy of Holies and sprinkled the blood seven times upon the mercy seat, and seven times before it.

So the high priest stood before the ark—typical of Christ—clothed in robes, typical of Christ's righteousness. Upon his bosom his breastplate set with twelve precious stones engraved with the names of the twelve tribes of Israel—typical of the abiding interest of all the Israel of God in the mediation of Christ—typical in expressing the truth that their names are imperishably engraven upon Christ's memory and heart.

"In his breastplate the Urim and Thummin—Urim signifying lights, Thummin signifying perfection—in virtue of which the priest gave oracular answers to the people, typical that God through Christ is the source of all experimentally religious knowledge and the infallible truth of salvation's plan as accomplished by the work of Christ and taught by His sacred lips and by the lips of others.

"Upon his brow a golden miter engraved with the phrase 'Holiness unto the Lord', typically testifying that perfect holiness was essential in a mediator between God and man, typically testifying that the coming Saviour would possess the required qualifications."

In his hand a censer of burning incense—typical of the intercessions of Christ and of God's great pleasure in a reconciliation with man through Christ.

This high priest stood sprinkling blood, the instrument of propitiation, upon the mercy seat.

The throne, the symbol of the being to be propitiated.

All typical of the expiatory nature and efficiency of the blood of Christ.

The high priest sprinkled the propitiatory blood upon the mercy seat, and before the mercy seat seven times—seven meaning perfection—typical of the perfect atonement to be made by Christ.

God instituted this sacrificial worship as typical.

Every sacrifice made before the flood, every sacrifice offered during the days of the patriarchs, every sacrifice offered by the Jews during all the years of Judaism—all were a type of Christ.

The crooked smoke that arose from Abel's altar, and the smoke from all the altars of Abraham and Noah and from the altars of the more diversified and systematic sacrifices of the Jews, gave evidence that the people were looking away by faith to the promised Seed, even Jesus.

Like finger-posts along the dusty highway of time, they pointed the faith of the worshipers to a sacrificial Saviour.

Types, they foreshadowed the great antitype. Adumbrations of a substance yet to come, significant shadows of redemptive entity still ahead, preparing and opening the way for something better through the rites imposing, through symbols splendid, through services sublime, these sacrifices were not ultimate but introductory.

The finishing of Christ's redemptive work on the Cross was the finishing of all these.

"It is finished," said Christ. And the vast system of the patriarchs and Judaism, colossal in structure, hoary in antiquity, passed away. Its altars dripping with blood drifted far into oblivion. For centuries, in shattered shreds upon the ruins of history, its priestly vestments have been flung.

Jesus, the great antitype, took all its rites, types, symbols, with Him to the Cross, and nailed them there. They died with Him. They were buried with Him. He rose. They did not.

"Nailing it to his Cross." (Colossians 2:14).

"The veil of the temple was rent in twain from the top to the bottom" (Matthew 27:51).

Meaning what? Meaning this: The Holy of Holies is

revealed in the Son of man. His altars are now manifest to all. In His salvation there are no priestly secrets. A child can learn His oracles. The old priesthood is superseded; the old sacrifices have lost their value and are absorbed in the one great sacrifice for sin. And because this one great sacrifice for sin, Jesus being both High Priest and Lamb of God, we say:

But beloved, we are persuaded better things of you, and things that accompany salvation (Hebrews 6:9).

Having therefore, brethren, boldness to enter into the holiest by the blood of Jesus (Hebrews 10:19).

And from Jesus Christ, who is the faithful witness, and the first begotten of the dead, and the prince of the kings of the earth. Unto him that loved us, and washed us from our sins in his own blood, and hath made us kings and priests unto God and his Father; to him be glory and dominion for ever and ever. Amen (Revelations 1:5, 6).

The types were redemption symbolized. The Christ redemption realized.

Yes, the ceremonial law with its mystic rites and interposed barriers was abrogated. The mercy seat, and the ark of the covenant with the broken tables of the law, and the pot of manna lay within the Holy of Holies. Now they stood revealed. Better still, they were charged with new meaning as these symbols were interpreted in the light of Christ's redemption. Henceforth the way to the Mercy Seat lay not through the sacrifice offered by human hands, but through the Lamb Himself.

All pointed to Jesus. Daniel tells when Christ will come. Micah where He will come from; Malachi of His forerunner. The Old Testament began with Christ, and it ends with Him. "The testimony of Jesus is the spirit of prophecy," says John. Jesus is the Alpha and Omega of the Bible, its animus, its mind, its spirit, the antitype of its types. He is the vital substance which gives meaning to its genealogies, meaning to its histories, meaning to its chronologies; the secret of its unity; the secret of its strength; the secret of its beauty.

III. THE DEBT OF SIN IS PAID

"It is finished."

The reality of sin and its deadly power makes the gravest problem with which human thought has ever grappled. Man in debt cannot pay out.

"Put that to mine account." That is, "It is finished" in other words!

By every thorn that punctured His brow, by every pang of pain, by every nail which pierced Him, by the savage Roman spear that drank from His side the precious libation of blood and water, by every drop of sinless blood shed that day, He said, "The debt is paid."

The debt paid, not with corruptible things such as silver and gold, from our vain manner of life handed down from our fathers, but with precious blood, as of a Lamb without blemish and without spot, even the blood of Jesus Christ paid the tribute money. There is exemption. There is redemption.

"It is finished." There is nothing further when everything is finished. He was the ripened fruit of the truth made under the law to redeem them that are under the law.

God has fully dealt for us with the law's claims that man shall deserve acceptance. Legal satisfaction is forever taken out of our hands by Christ. Christ Himself dealt, in the sinner's interest, with the law, honoring its holy claims to the uttermost under the human conditions which He freely undertook, so that, by faith, the community between Jesus and the sinner is real, the community of the sinner's debt on one side and Christ's merit on the other side.

The believer is complete in Him. The believer's hand

is free because Christ's was crushed. The believer's brow is painless because Christ's was bound. The believer's soul escapes because Christ's was bound. The believer gains heaven because Christ, for the believer, endured the torture and went through the horrors of hell. All the weapons of eternal wrath struck Him, but as they struck Him our race marched free.

"With his stripes we are healed." He died, not for His own sins, but for ours. He had no sin in Him. He humbled Himself that we might be exalted. He became poor that we might become rich. He was wounded that we might be healed. He drained the cup of wrath that we might drink the waters of salvation. For us and to pay our debt He came into the midst of earth's night to give light, into the midst of earth's sorrows to give joy, into the midst of earth's storm to give calm, into the midst of earth's death to give life, into the midst of earth's bondage to give liberty.

"Put that on mine account." Jesus paid the debt. God is just. He will not demand two payments for one debt. No. No honest man will demand two payments for one debt. No honest banker will demand two payments for one debt. Therefore. when I trust in Him, my debt is paid. All of it is paid!

> Jesus paid it all,
>   All to him I owe;
> Sin had left a crimson stain,
>   He washed it white as snow!

Every legal and philosophic condition involved in the nature of God, His attributes, system, government, law, in the nature of man, in man's relations and conditions and in the nature of things necessary to a perfect redemption, was fully met in the nature, character, work, sufferings, and death of Jesus!

My sins laid open the rod,
    And back which from the law was free,
And the Eternal Son of God,
    Received the stripes once due to me!

I pierced those sacred hands and feet
    That never touched or walked in sin,
I broke the heart that only beat,
    The souls of sinful men to win!

No beam was in his eye or mote,
    Nor laid to him was any blame,
And yet his cheeks for me were smote,
    The cheeks that never blushed for shame!

The sponge of vinegar and gall
    By me was placed under his tongue.
And when derision mocked his call,
    I stood that mocking crowd among.

And yet his blood was shed for me,
    To be of sin the double cure,
And balm there flows from Calvary's tree,
    That heals my guilt and makes me pure!

For every drunkard who will trust He says, "Put that on mine account." For every liar, every thief, every adulterer, every murderer He says, "Put that on mine account." There is exemption and there is redemption. There is nothing for us to do but to accept it through faith! But we must accept it. All the ceremonial sacrifices could not obtain the bond from the hand of the creditor. They were only acknowledgment of the debt. Jesus, by one offering, paid the whole, took up the bond, the handwriting that was against us, and nailed it to the Cross.

The statement, "It is finished", means

IV.   The Shadow of the Cross Lifted From Jesus

Earth has no darker sin, history has no blacker page, humanity has no fouler spot than that of the Saviour's crucifixion.

Jesus was born with the mark of the Cross upon His shoulders. With the weight of the Cross upon His heart, He learned to walk. With the weight of the Cross upon His shoulders, He learned to work. He bowed to baptism with the weight of the Cross upon Him. He endured temptation with the weight of the Cross upon Him. He began His ministry with the weight of the Cross upon Him. From His earliest moment it was His burden by day, His pallet by night. From Bethlehem into Egypt, with the shadow of the Cross upon Him, He went. From Egypt to Nazareth, with the shadow of the Cross upon Him, He went. He climbed Olivet oppressed by its weight. He walked the streets dishonored by its shame. He rose from the dead glorified by its sacrifice.

The Cross was with Him when they came with their lanterns and torches seeking the Light of the world. The Cross was with Him when Judas, with a kiss that burned His cheek like a hot sword, betrayed Him. The Cross was with Him when Annas asked Him concerning His disciples and doctrine. The Cross was with Him when Caiaphas condemned Him. The Cross was with Him when Herod mocked Him. The Cross was with Him when the people derided Him.

"The shadow of the Cross was on Bethlehem's swaddling clothes. The shadow of the Cross was on the road to Egypt. The shadow of the Cross was on the wall of the carpenter's shop. The shadow of the Cross was on opal and amethyst and emerald floor by Lake Galilee. The shadow of the Cross was on the well curb at Sychar. The shadow of the Cross was on the door of the temple. The shadow of the Cross was on the sunrise and sunset."

But now the shadow of the Cross is lifted. Never again shall He be persecuted from city to city, called a glutton and winebibber and a bastard and servant of Satan. Never again shall He sweat blood. Never again shall He say, "My soul is exceeding sorrowful unto death," and then go forth to a garden where the roots of His divine emotion put forth their crimson tears. Never again shall He be derided by the rabble. Never again shall He be spit upon and slapped and buffeted. Never again shall He be crowned with thorns. Never again shall He be lacerated with the scourge. Never again will He cry out in the anguish of His soul, "My God, my God, why hast thou forsaken me?"

On every path He walked, on every house He entered, on every city He visited was the shadow of the Cross which now, because of his death, is lifted.

V.   WHAT WAS FINISHED?

"It is finished!"

What was finished? Something has been accomplished. He hath finished the transgression and made reconciliation for iniquity, and brought in everlasting righteousness and sealed up the vision and the prophecy, and anointed a Holy of Holies!

The long list of prophecies beginning with Genesis 3:6, the Jewish economy of types and rituals, the work the Father had given Him to do, the matchless beauty of a perfect life, the claims of a broken law were all finished. Eternal justice was satisfied, righteousness vindicated, and heaven's throne established.

"Mercy and truth are met together; righteousness and peace have kissed each other" (Psalm 85:10).

Man's redemption is secured, and nothing left undone for man to do but to accept, receive, rejoice!

"It is finished!" At the transfiguration they spoke of a death which He would accomplish at Jerusalem. He has now reached the finishing touch. It is finished. Redemption is an accomplished fact.

There is no more to be done. This God-Man made one

sacrifice for sins forever, and sat down at the right hand of God.

The types are now all full.

The Old Testament pictures are now fulfilled. No more blood of bulls and goats on Jewish altars slain, no more burnt-offering, meal-offering, peace-offering, trespass-offering, sin-offerings. "By one offering he hath perfected forever."

No more lambs led to the slaughter, no more bullocks bound with cords to the horns of the altar of burnt offering, no more goats carried to the land of forgetfulness. No more shadows henceforth and forever.

When beginning His ministry He said, "I must be about my Father's business." Now He hath finished the transaction, and soon He will proclaim His triumph.

His meat was to do the will of God, which He hath done. It is finished. When work is done, rest follows. Why not accept the finished work and forever cease, except from the work which is sweet service to Him, whose sacrifice hath made thee whole?

What was finished? Redemption's completion! There it stood. The study of angels. The hope of men. The wonder of the universe. The crowning work of creation's God. The masterpiece of heaven! Finished!

What was finished? The abolishment of death for every believer. True, the Christian dies. But his death is no longer penal, but providential and provisional.

What was finished? The atonement, fundamental to salvation, is accomplished. As the bridge is fundamental to span the river, the foundation to the building, the blood fundamental to the body, the rails fundamental to the train, the mould fundamental to the pattern, the power fundamental to the car, the graft fundamental to alter the fruit, so Christ's atonement is fundamental to bring us to God, to rest our conscience in peace, to cause the life to function in the will of God, to keep our lives along the line of sacrifice, to mould us to die in the pattern of His sacrificial service, and to produce fruit unto holiness in the spirit of Him who loved us and gave Himself for us.

What was finished? The guilt and demerit of sin which induced the penalty of death have been set aside for all for whom the substitution avails. That is finished.

What was finished? The law that was hidden in His heart, as it was hidden in the ark of the covenant, was fulfilled to the letter. It was that complete fulfillment which found its accent in His cry on the Cross, "It is finished."

What was finished? Christ's intercourse with His disciples? No, for it was to be continued through forty wonderful days. Christ's preaching the Word of Life? No, for that was continued through the disciples who were to carry the Gospel to the ends of the earth. What then was finished, if not these things?

The great mission for which our Lord came to earth was finished, that for which the Son of God took on our human form and lived among men and died at last on the Cross—*that* was finished in the atonement for our sins. Finished was the age-long plan of salvation. Finally the Lamb was sacrificed, slain by anticipation from the foundation of the world. Completed was God's sacrificial purpose for His creatures. Finished the proof and standing evidence of divine love, held up forever, nailed to the bloody cross!

Well might Jesus cry, "It is finished." And now let every grateful life respond, "In my heart and in my life it is begun!"

What was finished? His "gory crown was changed to a glory crown." May we not say that which brought the gory was the glory? If there had been no gory crown, there could have been no glory crown.

What was finished? God's announcement by the voice

of the prophets that the old covenant was obliterated and abrogated and that a new covenant was here. The blood of animals sprinkled upon stubborn heads, upon blaspheming faces, had lost its virtue—another blood, pure and precious, was "drawn from Immanuel's veins."

What was finished? The hour for which He came into the world had run its course. The cup which with such a trembling hand He had put to shrinking lips has been drunk to its dregs. The powers of darkness have made on Him, amid furies of earth and the hatreds of hell, their last assault and, though they know it not, have been repelled. The momentary darkness of His Father's countenance has passed away.

What was finished? "'Tis done, the great transaction is done." The perfect fulfillment of all the law required is finished.

What was finished? There was finished upon the Cross the new, the full, the wonderful revelation of the Father, that unbosoming of the Eternal, the opening up to us of the very heart of the Godhead, the exhibition of the mingled love and holiness of our Father who is in heaven. There was completed then that glorious, that attractive, that subduing manifestation of the love of God for sinful men, which carried the Divine Being to the extreme length of suffering and of self-sacrifice, and which has ever formed the most powerful of all instruments of pacifying the conscience, melting the heart, moulding the character, renewing and sanctifying the will.

What was finished? Whatever obstacles our guilt threw in the way of our being received back into the divine favor, have been removed. Whatever the integrity of His law, and the moral interests of His government required in the way of atonement or expiation, has been rendered. The way of access to God is lying open to us. That is what was meant when Jesus said, "It is finished," amid the darkness and blood of Calvary's hill.

That is what is meant now when, amid the quiet of our homes, we read the story of the Cross. All our guilt is buried, buried beyond being raised again, in the depths of His atonement.

Finished! It seemed the finishing of Him—an inglorious defeat. Three years of ministry. A bribed disciple. An arrest at midnight. Pilate washing his hands of guilty blood. A cross swaying in the darkness with a white blood-splotched naked body upon it, and earthquake, and a burial.

But at last, human history unrolls its vast scroll! The scene is ablaze with light. The voices of the prophets swell into thunder peals of triumph. Mount Sinai kneels before Calvary. The Occident takes the place of the Orient in the march of the ages, and seated upon the world's throne is the Christ, the revolutions and reformations of twenty centuries, the wonders of modern civilization, attesting the glories of His triumphs. King— all hail! Wonderful!

United States history records the building of a great transcontinental railway line which would unite the country by rail from the Atlantic to the Pacific.

During the construction financial embarrassment overtook the promoters, and with difficulty they secured the funds. There was rejoicing when the work was resumed. The day came when the last rail was to be laid on the border line between New Mexico and Colorado. It was planned to be a great event. A special order was sent to California for a laurel wood tie, and two silver spikes were ordered—one for Colorado and one for New Mexico. The governor of each State was invited. They were to drive the two silver spikes into the laurel wood tie, thus completing the work of construction, making a way of transportation from ocean to ocean and binding together the two States.

As the governors drove the two silver spikes into the

laurel tie, the great crowd applauded, and a tapped telegraph wire bore the news with a flash out to the entire country and world! It was a great feat and accomplishment.

There was a day when four spikes were driven, not into a laurel tie, but into the cursed tree and through the hands and feet of the Son of God!

They were not spikes of silver, but of iron and steel and driven while heaven, earth and underearth looked on. Then the last spike was driven, a shout went up from all the creation—the news flashed to the ends of the world, for a way of transportation from sin and its darkness had been completed! "It is finished" was the cry!

The way was now open from earth to heaven! There was a trail to the end! A means of access to God had been completed! The spikes were not driven by friends, but by enemies, for it was while we were yet enemies, Christ died for us! The last spike driven through the hands of the son of God on the rugged Cross brought man and God together! It was a reconciling death! It was a peace-making transaction! The bonded indebtedness was now fully met and the debt was paid.

It was on a certain day in the reign of Tiberius that the bond fell due. The Holy One and the Just One came forward in surety and cried "Set that to mine account." He climbed that Cross, that cursed tree, with an unforced will! He yielded His hands to those spikes of iron. From the spike of iron came forth the "rod of iron" with which He will yet rule the nations! "O glorious transaction, 'tis done." Shout it, sound it forth, cry aloud, the way to God is an open way! "It is finished!"

PRINTED IN THE UNITED STATES OF AMERICA.